THE COMPLETE CORPORATE COACHING TOOLKIT

The **QUINTESSENTIAL GUIDE** *for* **21ST CENTURY BUSINESS COACHES** *and* **LEADERS**

MONICA JONSSON A.M.C.

ISBN : 9798763361834

Edited by Andrea Murphy - www.perfectwordsmith.com
Cover image and layout: IDDI FIX - www.iddifix.lu
Imprint: Independently published

This book is dedicated to my husband, Mario, for his love, support and encouragement in its writing, and to my son, Theo, in the sincere hope that he will one day live in a world that is inclusive of everyone: where *all human beings have equal value, equal rights and equal opportunity*.

Acknowledgements

My heartfelt thanks go to:

My clients, who continue to be my greatest teachers.

Barbara Cormack and Gerard O'Donovan for their invaluable advice and support when I was setting up my coaching practice during a time when there were no other coaches or accreditation bodies in Luxembourg.

Curly Martin, Ian McDermott, Robert Dilts, Sir John Whitmore, Stephen Covey, Michael Grinder and John Whittington, for the privilege of attending their first-class courses and being inspired by their vast knowledge, wisdom and experience.

The pre-readers of this book: Carin Junestrand, Nastja Raabe, Brandi Karlstedt, Anita Jonsson, Alberta Brusi, Madelene Gorbutt, Eva Holmqvist, Peter Mullen, Jean Marc Crépin and Dawn Campbell for giving their precious time and feedback.

Nastja Raabe and Brandi Karlstedt for their kind foreword.

My Editor, Andrea Murphy - the perfect wordsmith.

And last but by no means least, my grandmother Harriet and mother Anita for being role models in pioneering female empowerment by their own example.

Thank You!

Foreword

Throughout life's journey, we hope to cross paths with those who inspire, see the potential in us and in others and drive positive change. These are the key attributes of being an effective coach - and a perfect description of Monica Jonsson. We say this confidently, as we have had both the pleasure and privilege of working with her.

We first met Monica individually while in corporate roles and studying to become coaches. We embraced her elegant approach to ensuring a successful outcome for all parties, from the very outset of the goal-setting and right through the committed coaching sessions.

Later, when we worked with her under the CoachDynamix umbrella, our eyes were opened to how she had developed her toolkit over the course of thousands of coaching hours: with leaders, executives, managers and teams in a diverse range of organisations. When we started using these tools in our own coaching practices, we quickly found that our coachees had far greater support and thus better focus throughout their coaching journey; and as new coaches, we were reminded of many important guiding principles that as humans we can easily forget in this busy world. With these resources and Monica's insights, we were perfectly armed to build impactful, trusted coaching relationships and experience our own personal and professional growth that happily continues today.

And now, with this toolkit, you will be perfectly armed too.

Our wish for you is to enjoy Monica's gifts of wisdom and knowledge as much as we do.

Nastja Raabe
Brandi Karlstedt

CONTENTS

Introduction 12

About this Book 15

My Discovery of Coaching 17

Part 1: About Coaching **21**

The Coaching Process 24

The Art of Coaching 32

Coaching and the Corporate World 38

**Part 2: The Corporate Coaching
Toolkit** **41**

Introducing the Corporate Coaching Toolkit.............. 44

Leadership **47**

About Leadership **48**

General Leadership Skills................................*51*

1.1 What Makes a Good Leader?..................... 52

1.2 Self-Awareness 56

1.3 What do you Value? 60

1.4 Six Leadership Styles................................. 64

1.5 Self-Reflection... 68

1.6 Role Clarification 72

1.7 Strategic Thinking 76

1.8 Leader Qualities 80

Leading the Team...*85*

1.9 Leading the Team 86

1.10 Situational Leadership 90

1.11 Solution Orientation 94

1.12 One-to-One Coaching Meetings 98

1.13 Team Meetings 102

1.14 Team Meetings Assessment 106

1.15 Coaching-Style Questions 110

1.16 Developing the Team 114

1.17 Delivering Feedback 118

1.18 Preparing a Feedback Conversation 122

1.19 Leading Remotely...................................126

1.20 Communicating in Uncertainty 130

Effective Communication **133**

About Effective Communication................**134**

2.1 The Communication Process 136

2.2 Perception..140

2.3 Reflecting about Communication.............144

2.4 Nonverbal Communication.......................148

2.5 Levels of Listening...................................152

2.6 Rapport 156

2.7 Inclusive Language 160

2.8 Assertiveness..164

2.9 Communicating Assertively......................168

2.10 Useful Assumptions about Communication 172

Emotional Intelligence **175**

About Emotional Intelligence **176**

3.1 EI Model 180

3.2 Self-Awareness and Self-Management
(EI Model)...184

3.3 Reflecting on Real Events 190

3.4 Empathy 194

3.5 Meta Mirror 198

Stakeholder Management.......................... **201**

About Stakeholder Management **202**

4.1 Stakeholder/Power Map...........................204

4.2 Stakeholder Analysis 208

4.3 Personal Brand 212

4.4 Concrete Actions 216

Influencing and Negotiation **219**

About Influencing and Negotiation...........**220**

5.1 Win-Win Mindset...................................... 222

5.2 Six-Step Strategy 226

Personal Efficiency and Effectiveness...................**229**

About Personal Efficiency and Effectiveness........**230**

6.1 Eisenhower Matrix....................................232

6.2 Checkpoint 236

6.3 Effective Delegation.................................240

6.4 Assess 244

6.5 Aide-Mémoire...248

Life Balance **251**

About Life Balance **252**

7.1 Current Situation 254

7.2 What is Important to You? 258

7.3 Desired Life Balance 262

Appendix **265**

Coaching Questions....................................**266**

Resources..**269**

About the Author **270**

"Diversity is being invited to the party; inclusion is being asked to dance."

Verna Myers

Introduction

Each and every one of us has more influence than we may realise. Time and again we witness how 'ordinary' people inspire countless others to act - and how in their quest to raise social awareness they may be propelled into becoming unexpected leaders. One such ordinary yet extraordinary young woman is Greta Thunberg, who in 2018 demonstrated just how influential a single person can be. At the age of just fifteen, Greta started a global movement by sitting alone outside the Swedish parliament with a sign that read *School Strike for Climate*. In her determination to save our planet, she continues to fervently message world leaders, forums and powerful individuals to wake up, understand the urgency and act now. Her courage, leadership and impact earned her recognition in Forbes' list of *The World's 100 Most Powerful Women* (2019), Time magazine's *100 Most Influential People* and their youngest *Person of the Year* (2019), as well as two nominations for the Nobel Peace Prize (2019 and 2020). Impressive, inspirational and humbling, to say the least - and it all serves as testament to the title of one of her books: *No One is Too Small to Make a Difference*.

Individually we may not be able to save the world, but we can all choose to act on matters close to our hearts, in however small or large ways. And when we do, the ripple effect can be considerable.

This makes me think of Captain Sir Thomas Moore, affectionately known as Captain Tom, who in the midst of the COVID-19 pandemic set out to raise £1,000 for the UK's National Health Service charities by walking a hundred 25-metre lengths of his garden. In just twenty-four days he raised a staggering £32.8 million and was knighted by The Queen on his 100th birthday. Stories like his and Greta's inspire hope and action.

Viewing things from this perspective helps shift our thinking towards possibilities and opportunities that nurture our determination and desire to act. Goal clarity, self-empowerment, commitment and action are at the very core of coaching, and I consider it such a privilege to witness first-hand the extraordinary things my clients achieve when these elements and this mindset are in play.

Coaching is a profession in the service of others and has the potential to be a phenomenal force for good. For me personally, in my role as corporate coach, it is a means of doing my part to contribute to a workplace that is kinder, more human and above all inclusive. It is my conviction that corporate cultures which are defined by 'humanness' will outperform those which are not, and that this will be key to building future-proof businesses. I remain hopeful for a universal transformation of the corporate business world: where leadership unites rather than divides people around purposeful ambitions; where collaboration is the *modus operandi*; where people can feel safe and well and motivated to bring their whole selves to work. My purpose and passion is to contribute to this vision: to help create a positive ripple effect by coaching senior executives and leadership teams.

The corporate workplace is rapidly moving into what is sometimes referred to as the age of 'QuadGen', where four generations - the so-called Baby Boomers, Generation X, Millennials (or Gen Y) and now Generation Z - will need to co-exist. A slew of global research compiled over recent years concludes that the expectations of knowledge workers have changed. Findings reveal that they are looking for purpose, meaning and fulfilment at work, and that these personal identity-related aspects are more important than ever before. Employees want to feel respected and valued, experience a sense of belonging and be treated fairly. They want the opportunity to develop their skills, make an impact and have greater flexibility and freedom to lead balanced lives. It is noteworthy that these motivational factors are distinctly *intrinsic* rather than *extrinsic* (based on remuneration or reward); and to be relevant and attractive, companies need to be mindful to strike a good balance between the two. What is more, generational differences are not always as big as we may think: the above examples are desires common across all four generations.

Business leaders and senior executives often ask: "Why are our employee engagement survey results not where we want them to be?" and "Why is it so hard to attract and retain talent?" Even with the rapid rate of progress company structures, norms and rules designed by men for men in the early to mid-1900s have remained fairly static, despite an increasingly diverse workforce - particularly women - joining in significant numbers in the last fifty or so years. Thus the corporate environment is often seen as challenging for many 'newcomers', who experience no real sense of belonging or of being valued. Exclusion and/or micro-aggressions of certain employee groups rooted in bias is not uncommon, and because human beings are wired for inclusion this has a real impact on well-being, trust, engagement and performance. Gallup's most recent *State of the Workplace* report[1] shows that 85% of the global workforce feels disengaged at work. There is a clear disconnect between today's corporate cultures and employees' expectations about what life at work should be. Not only is this sad, but it is also unsustainable as we are witnessing with the unprecedented global phenomenon referred to as the 'Great Resignation'.

It may sound cliché but people really are an organisation's most valuable and important asset. It is the personnel, through their dedication, motivation, creativity and hard work, who determine the level of success and sustainability of an organisation. Again, it is well documented that employees' engagement is strongly linked to the sense of inclusion they feel at work. According to a recent McKinsey & Co survey[2], inclusion has become a central criterion as today's workforce plan their careers - to the point where 39% of the surveyed respondents reported having rejected a job because of a perceived lack of inclusion at the organisation. If attracting and retaining talent is high on the strategic agenda, then leaders need to acknowledge this perceptional mismatch and prioritise creating company cultures where all employees feel that they belong, they are valued and they can thrive.

To remain competitive and relevant in a world that has become truly global, a diverse representation - ethnicity, gender, sexual orientation, generation - at all levels is a necessity. Not only is this a matter of fairness, but it is also imperative for an organisation's continuous learning, innovation, value creation, growth and prosperity. Our greatest strength resides in our differences: we complement each other with our multitude of qualities, skills, talents; with our variegated cultures, perspectives and ideas. Collectively we are smart and therefore need each other to achieve greatness. However, this can only be achieved by adopting a corporate mindset and culture that is *inclusive of everyone* - where there is psychological safety and trust. It is easy to 'talk a good game' about the value of diversity, but without efforts to actively dispel conscious and unconscious bias, or solid actions behind the words, progress will remain slow. Viewing things from a macro-perspective, grass-root movements-turned-global like #MeToo and #BlackLivesMatter (BLM) are tirelessly advocating for inclusion and greatly accelerating this much-needed change across all areas of our societies. For the first time since 1968, people across the world are joining together in protest against injustices - this time to show their active support for the BLM movement in a call for unity: that *all human beings have equal value* and should therefore have equal rights and opportunity.

In an ever-changing business landscape where 'good' is no longer good enough, there is huge pressure on companies to deliver world-class products and services with demonstrable efficiency, innovation and exceptional client service. To navigate successfully through these challenges, current leadership practices based on old rules and bureaucratic legacies must be replaced by human-centred principles that comprise purpose, trust, engagement and creativity. Moreover, this can no longer remain in the hands of the one

---

1 State of the Global Workplace: 2021 Report, Gallup
2 *Understanding organisational barriers to a more inclusive workplace*, June 2020

'heroic' leader at the top of the house. Managers at all levels of an organisation need to do their part to foster cultures that enable high-performing workforces to deliver on these challenges.

I find that many leaders these days understand (at least intellectually) the importance of inclusive and purpose-led organisations, and that an excessive focus on profits usually leads to employee disengagement; yet they struggle to adapt existing models to lead and operate this way. However, since no two companies are the same, there is no single template that will work for all situations. Every leader and leadership team needs to become more reflective, both individually and as a whole, to figure out what this means for their business and how to transform their organisation for the better.

One silver lining of COVID-19 has been the opportunity it has given companies to re-evaluate how they currently operate. The largest remote working experiment ever undertaken has provided valuable take-aways to consider in determining what the 'future of work' in business might be. It has offered a chance to emerge from the crisis with updated, leading-edge work environments that give employees the means to achieve both their own and their organisation's goals, led by a new breed of leaders who inspire and show the way by their own example.

This will be crucial to build future-proof, sustainable businesses that can successfully meet the demands and challenges of the 21st century and beyond.

About this Book

In the process of becoming a coach, I probably also became one of Amazon's best customers. My bookshelves are packed with coaching guides and manuals from a vast range of perspectives, all of which have greatly contributed to advancing my knowledge as a coach practitioner.

However, early on in my career coaching executives, I realised something was missing in providing them with some level of context and content for recurring soft skills topics such as leadership, emotional intelligence and effective communication. Even though soft skills are intellectually easy to understand, the process of integrating them to improve one's proficiency is notably less straightforward. It was clear that a lack of substance for these abstract topics made it harder than necessary for clients to work on them.

I concluded that a toolkit providing the right level of context and content for the soft skills most in demand by executives would help advance learning and development, and thereby be a great companion to the coaching process. Such a toolkit would better equip executives to turn their understanding into meaningful actions and accelerate progress towards their desired goals, providing a well-rounded and lasting support that would extend beyond the coaching conversation. Yet when searching for this type of toolkit, I never found one that really met my expectations. So in the end, I decided the best way forward would be to create the tools I was looking for myself.

The Corporate Coaching Toolkit presented in this book has been created for one-to-one coaching with executives ranging from CEO to manager level. It is designed to advance learning and development, to encourage meaningful reflection, to develop self-awareness and to help determine suitable actions - enabling executives to be more successful in their roles.

The Toolkit has been developed drawing on experiences from my own international corporate career, invaluable insights from client assignments, coaching-related courses and ongoing research into latest trends and findings in the soft skills and corporate domains. It is a comprehensive collection of practical, pragmatic and powerful tools that cover the most popular soft skills topics in the corporate environment, and it has been designed with two audiences in mind:

1. Professional coaches working in the corporate/business space who wish to be more effective and impactful in coaching their clients. Here the tools provide a perfect complement to the coaching conversation and overall coaching assignment.

2. Executives who prefer to develop their own soft skills unaccompanied and be their own 'coach'. For these executives, the Toolkit will offer great support to help increase their aptitude, make steady progress and amplify the coaching component of their leadership.

Since the primary aim of this book is to share the Toolkit, I will not be covering all the fundamentals of coaching. There are so many great books out there defining and describing the core principles, detailing the different coaching methodologies and approaches, laying out the business of coaching and how to set up your own practice. However, I do cover some of the basics that I consider critical to deliver best-practice coaching.

The book has two main parts and is structured as follows.

Part 1 includes:
- *The Coaching Process,* which provides a thorough description of its main parts: Goal, Action Plan, Feedback and Learning.
- *The Art of Coaching,* which answers the question "What makes a great coach?"
- *Coaching and the Corporate World,* which gives a brief overview of the distinctive role that coaching can play in this domain.

Part 2 begins with a general introduction to position the Toolkit followed by the Toolkit itself, which includes the following seven soft skills topics:
- Leadership
- Effective Communication
- Emotional Intelligence
- Stakeholder Management
- Influencing and Negotiation
- Personal Efficiency and Effectiveness
- Life Balance

Developed over 12,000 coaching hours with hundreds of executives in numerous organisations across multiple industries, the tools in the book have been thoroughly tested and are now ready for you to start using.

My Discovery of Coaching

The first time I came across coaching outside a sporting context was in 2002 in a random shop in London, where I happened to pick up a brochure with the word *coaching* on it. An exhilarating sensation washed over me and my heart started to race. I couldn't understand why I was having such strong reaction to a word I didn't really know the meaning of, and naturally my curiosity was ignited to find out more. Subsequent research left me beyond inspired and wishing that *I* could have benefited from external coaching in my own corporate career - particularly in the more senior positions.

At that point in my life I had been longing for a professional change for a while, but had no idea what such a change could be. I loved many aspects of my work, but the truth is I was growing increasingly tired of stagnant company cultures that did not value diversity - either of people or of thought - as well as the more unpleasant side of corporate politics that seemed to accelerate with every promotion. This had left me so drained that one day I realised I had 'lost my mojo'. I found myself longing to be engaged in something that felt meaningful; to have a more comprehensive, positive impact; to be a force for good in some way.

Coaching resonated strongly with me for several factors:
- Its mission to empower and support people to harness their unique greatness and create the life they desire.
- Its focus on goal-orientation and constructive action.
- Its advocacy for humanity, unity, inclusion and collaboration.
- Its central principle that no two persons or organisations are the same and that therefore there is no 'one size fits all' solution for developing skills, building strategies and sharpening performance.

Quite unexpectedly, I had found the professional change I was looking for!

I decided to abandon a successful corporate career and re-focus all my energy on getting qualified and accredited as a professional coach. Then in 2003 I set up the very first coaching company in Luxembourg: CoachDynamix[3].

Given my background, it was natural for corporate coaching to become the core business of my practice. My aspiration was to reach out to the most senior executives, being fully aware that any transformation towards kinder, more human-centric and more inclusive company cultures must begin at the top.

Within a few weeks of making the decision to become a coach I got my first client. I was talking about my new-found ambition with someone at a party and I guess my enthusiasm must have been contagious, because before I knew it he said, "Wow, that's great and it's exactly what I need. I have just been promoted to Director and I feel rather lost; when can we start?" I thought, "Oh my goodness, I'm not ready yet!" But this thought was quickly replaced by another: "This is your chance to start - take it!" I decided to listen to the second thought and to interpret what had just happened as a sign that I was on the right track.

An interesting experience in completely changing my professional direction was witnessing first-hand how unsettling this was for those around me, and understanding their picture of how I should fit into their world. I was astonished and completely unprepared for some of the negative reactions I received from people I considered to be close friends.

---

3 http://coachdynamix.com/

Firstly, there was a general strong scepticism about coaching in general and that it was surely only a short-lived trend. Secondly, how could I give up the career I had built and throw myself into something so uncertain? And thirdly (my favourite one): Who did I think I was to believe that I could coach others?! As if my own fears and doubts and trying to deal with them weren't enough, it seemed that almost everyone around me thought I was making a huge mistake!

During this time, I was often torn between opposing feelings of great enthusiasm and great fear, all of which were new to me. In my corporate career I had consistently challenged myself by taking on brand new roles and responsibilities, and embracing the opportunity for growth that they provided. But this project was different and full of uncertainty.

I decided to spend an entire day by myself, leaning in to my fear and really listening to the thoughts running through my head: what it would mean to give up the career I had invested so much of myself into, the attractive financial package, the benefits and security of being an employee; to no longer have an established corporate brand behind me with all the advantages that represents. Was I prepared to give all of that up to pioneer something nobody even knew about? What if the others were right? Was this all just a naïve dream? This may be a good place to mention that I was also expecting a baby(!) So was I crazy to make this move..?

At the end of that day, I took a deep breath, closed my eyes, went inside and asked myself: "OK, with all these fears on the table is this still what you want to do?" The answer came to me in an instant and was a resounding YES! And from that moment I decided to surround myself with people who would be supportive of my coaching project. Finally my thinking was clear. Any other way would simply bring additional obstacles on a road that was already challenging and scary.

Now this didn't mean that I never experienced fears and doubts again: these thoughts came and went, but I took consistent actions to eliminate any additional fuel for my negative/fearful thinking.

It's our negative/fearful thoughts that make us doubt ourselves and our capabilities. I am sure you recognise some of these:

- *I can't do that!*
- *I will probably fail*
- *I don't have the right background*
- *I'm not smart enough*
- *I'm not talented enough*
- *I'm too old*
- *I'm too young*
- *I'm not rich enough*

And the list goes on....

These thoughts all have an element of "I'm not good enough" attached to them. Fear of failure is probably the most common one, and it is often what holds us back from even trying in the first place. However, we tend to forget that *there is no courage without fear*. Setbacks are part of life and through them there is usually opportunity to develop and grow - if we are open to learn. This becomes evident when we read the biographies of highly successful people and see how these people probably experience failure and setback more than most. Central to their success is that they use those setbacks as opportunities to learn and then incorporate that knowledge to try again.

When we can identify our negative or limiting thoughts and beliefs and proactively work on replacing them with supportive beliefs, we have a brand new playing field. We empower ourselves and take control of our situation. We feel the spark of aliveness within us.

To start any business - and in particular to pioneer a brand new business sector - takes big doses of courage, drive, discipline and perseverance; because having a good idea and being passionate about it is not enough: setting up and running your own organisation requires a lot of hard and focused work. There are moments of great triumph and there are moments when you just want to give up, but the key is to keep going when the going gets tough and never give up what you believe in. Success does not happen overnight: it happens one step at a time; and it is important to take consistent actions, no matter how small, and to keep moving forward.

I often highlight how essential it is to have people around who believe in us - even if it is just one person. My biggest supporter during those challenging times was my husband Mario, whose unwavering support continues to be invaluable to this day. During the course of 2002/2003, my belly grew as my coaching project advanced, and my beautiful baby boy Theo and my coaching practice CoachDynamix were born within a few months of each other.

This was transformative for me on both accounts. Becoming a parent teaches us numerous things, including selflessness and patience; it develops our capacity for empathy and the importance of being present in the moment; and above all it shows us the true meaning of unconditional love. Becoming a coach marked the start of another brand new journey filled with more learning, insights, joy, challenges and a renewed sense of purpose.

Close to twenty years on, I remain passionate and incredibly grateful for the opportunity to positively contribute to my clients' journeys through the force for good that coaching enables. It is truly amazing to observe what people can achieve when trust, support and the tools to succeed are extended to them.

On that note, I would like to end on a favourite quote by Henry Ford:

"Whether you believe you can do a thing or not, you are right."

PART 1

ABOUT COACHING

"I believe that wherever there is mastery, coaching is occurring, and whenever coaching is done, mastery will be the outcome."

Andrea J. Lee

The Coaching Process

The role of a sports coach working alongside athletes is well established: every successful athlete has a coach. Coaching in other domains, such as corporate and life coaching, has been developed around many of the same principles used in sports - in particular its focus on goals, performance and outcomes.

The Coaching Partnership

One-to-one coaching is a distinctive partnership between two people connected in humanity - coach and coachee - who work together as equals on a defined set of coachee goals. It is a confidential and in-depth dialogue aimed at deepening a coachee's self-awareness and clarity.

Albert Einstein allegedly defined insanity as doing the same thing over and over again and expecting a different outcome. However, even though we all understand this concept, we also know that it is not always easy to abandon certain deep-rooted patterns. As such coaching empowers, encourages and challenges the coachee to think differently, think bigger; and holds them accountable to reach their goals faster than they would do on their own. It provides a safe space to explore with an external coach who has no emotional attachment or vested interest in organisational politics and can therefore act as an objective sparring partner and sounding board.

This is often of critical value to people in leadership positions as they seldom receive honest input from the people below them. Leadership expert Warren Bennis found in his work with thousands of executives that 70% of followers would not give their frank opinion if it was at odds with their superior - even if they were certain that superior was about to make a mistake. Bennis referred to this as 'the 70% factor'. A good coach will ask the challenging questions that enable leaders to really reflect on themselves and to thoroughly contemplate strategies and consequences of potential decisions.

A central principle that emphasises coaching's capacity to empower is that people often have the answers and wisdom within; they may simply not have asked themselves the right questions. In this dynamic partnership, the coach listens and asks the relevant questions which lead to broader perspectives, new and fresh insights and better decisions. This in turn enables the coachee to enhance and/or develop a broader range of behaviours and skills, so that they may be more effective in managing themselves and their relationships with others while remaining genuine and authentic.

Enhancing a skill (as opposed to developing one) is about refreshing or sharpening aspects of something we are already good at. As an example, a leadership style that has served us well in the past may turn out to be somewhat outdated in view of changes in employee and business demands, and may therefore need updating in order to be inspiring, relevant and effective. Another example can be taking oneself from being a good public speaker to becoming an outstanding one.

When describing the coaching partnership I like to use the metaphor of a dance, where the coachee leads and the coach follows that lead. This means that there may be times when you, as coach, have prepared a coaching session to take a certain direction, only to realise that your coachee's agenda has unexpectedly changed, requiring you to adjust your course elegantly and seamlessly.

The Coaching Process

There is nothing complicated about coaching. Quite the contrary: it's a pretty straightforward and pragmatic process. However, explaining it to others in a concise manner can be somewhat of a challenge, as most new coaches discover when seeking to passionately convey the power of the practice. Even though the overall understanding of coaching has greatly improved over the years, it has also become one of the most popular business buzzwords; and as a buzzword it is used in a variety of contexts where assumptions and perceptions can vary. Shortly after launching my coaching practice, I created the following illustration as a visual aid to explain the coaching process. Explaining the process and clarifying any questions the coachee may have at the outset of an assignment is key for good collaboration: it ensures alignment between both parties and sets the right expectations from the start.

The Coaching Process

Awareness · Brainstorm · Strategy · Implement · Stakeholders · Self · Coach · Result · Transformation · Learning · Action Plan · Feedback · GOAL

© CoachDynamix®

Inside the Coaching Process

Goal, Action Plan, Feedback and Learning

Goal

The goal (or goals) is at the heart of coaching, which is why it is positioned at the very centre of the illustration. Helping the coachee gain clarity about what they really want is one of the most important parts of the process, because defining clear and concise goals is not always as straightforward as it may appear.

In today's fast-paced world it is not uncommon that we leap into action mode before being clear about what we actually want to achieve. Many of us live with great pressure, both professionally and privately: we feel restless, with an urge to be constantly productive, which means we often don't stop to think things through. However, actions simply for the sake of actions can result in undesired consequences, and so we do well to regularly slow down, take a step back and ask ourselves what is important *now*.

Most of us know with great certainty what we don't want and can easily speak about this for hours, but when engaging in these kinds of conversations we will most likely be in a problem-oriented frame of mind. This is not conducive to thinking about goals because it activates the 'avoidance' part of our brain. The role of the coach in this phase is to help the coachee reframe their thinking by asking questions that open up the mind to new perspectives and possibilities; that trigger curiosity, discovery, a sense of excitement and creativity. By shifting the coachee's attention, the coach helps activate the coachee's 'moving towards' function in the brain, which is the optimal place to be when seeking goal clarity. So although it is easy to know what we *don't* want, we tend to struggle to clearly articulate the answer when faced with questions like: "And what would you like to have happen?" "What specifically are you looking to achieve?" or "What would the ideal situation be?"

Since the goal drives the rest of the process, defining a clear and concise goal needs to be the starting point of any coaching journey. I will spend the entire first session with the coachee exploring and defining specific goals, to consider the purpose (the 'Why?') behind them, and what will it bring the coachee by achieving them.

Here are a few examples of how corporate coaching goals may be formulated:

- *Sharpen my leadership skills to build a performing team that is competent, engaged and collaborative and works together towards the same vision.*

- *Take myself and the team to the next level by stepping away from details, allowing others to evolve and myself to focus increasingly on strategy and active leadership.*

- *Learn to communicate effectively and facilitate different expectations with the objective of finding alignment among stakeholders.*

- *Strengthen relationships with my key internal stakeholders to increase my visibility and have meaningful strategic exchanges with them.*

- *Organise my priorities and time in such a way that I can minimise procrastination and successfully meet deadlines.*

I like to think about each goal as a lighthouse shining the way ahead: it is my job as coach to regularly bring the coachee's attention back to its beam, ensuring we remain focused and on track. Depending on the situation, I might ask questions such as:
- "Are we working on the relevant points to get you where you want to be?"
- "Is something missing?"
- "How important is this goal to you as things currently stand?"

Once the goal(s) has been defined, there are three points to be included that are of utmost importance. These are: identifying success factors; agreeing on a target date for assessing progress; and verifying the coachee's level of commitment.

Success Factors

How people measure success can differ quite a bit. To give a simple example, a coachee's goal may be to improve their leadership skills. Depending on the person, role and situation, success factors for that goal could be one or more of the following:
- achieving buy-in for the vision
- increasing employee engagement
- finding their leadership voice
- developing ownership in their team

- getting promoted
- feeling accepted by the peer group

Consequently, clarifying a coachee's success factors becomes necessary in order to assess progress. Similar to defining goals, finding the success factors can be challenging for the coachee and may require some deeper probing on the part of the coach. I find that a good way to stimulate this thought process is to read the exact goal formulation out loud to them and then let them finish the sentence: "I know that I have made good progress when........"

Target Date

When measuring progress made on soft skills goals, it is not possible to assign the same kind of key performance indicators (KPIs) as is typically done to measure technical/hard goals. This is why setting precise target dates to regularly assess progress is critical. Target dates serve as a catalyst for action and an upcoming checkpoint for tracking progress made.

It is important to note that working on soft skills is about making steady progress, as opposed to their being completely achieved and therefore ticked off the list. If we want to improve our leadership skills, this is probably not something we work on just once and then consider accomplished: it is an ongoing process where we can continue to make progress for as long as we are in a leadership position.

Commitment

As we all know, when we set ourselves a goal our commitment to achieve it is absolutely fundamental: the greater our commitment, the greater the likelihood of success. And the opposite is of course also true: if our commitment is low, we will not perform as well as we could. We may even fail.

Coaching will only succeed when there is a strong commitment on the part of the coachee to put in the work necessary to achieve their goals. The progress made will be in direct relation to work done, and this is something that I always highlight at the outset of a coaching assignment: "What you put into the coaching is what you will get out of it."

If I suspect a coachee's level of commitment is not sufficiently high, then I test it. I typically use a scale of 1 to 10 (10 being the highest) to do this. I will read the goal out loud and then ask questions such as:
- "On this scale, where are you?"
- "How important is this to you?"
- "What is it going to take to make it a 10?"

In my experience, the coachee's level of commitment needs to be at least an 8 to be worth working on. If the level is below 8, then the reason for this needs to be explored; and the goal formulation may need to be adjusted for the coachee to really commit. This is a key piece of the coaching journey where the coach needs to hold the coachee accountable.

Action Plan

Once the goal(s) has been defined, the process moves to the *Action Plan* phase. This is where we brainstorm different options, clarify personalised strategies and agree actions to be implemented by the coachee. Since everyone is unique, strategies and actions can vary tremendously from one coachee to the next.

In this phase of the coaching I often use the phrase *Doing is Understanding*. This expresses the importance of taking one's intellectual knowledge and turning it into concrete actions to also get the experiential knowledge - in other words, acquiring a complete understanding.

When it comes to soft skills, we learn by practice and repetition. This is how we integrate intellectual knowledge and, most importantly, how we make lasting progress. The more frequently a new way of thinking or behaving is repeated, the stronger the underlying circuits in our brains become. With practice and repetition we create and strengthen new pathways between neurons, and are literally able to rewire our brains.

It is therefore not sufficient merely to have interesting and thought-provoking conversations: these conversations must be followed by real actions to make steady progress. A simple example illustrates this and also encapsulates Mr. Einstein's quote above: you can read a lot of great books about leadership and attend a multitude of classes, but unless you do something different you will not enhance your leadership skills.

Feedback

Once new/alternative actions and behaviours have been implemented, the process moves to the *Feedback* phase. Feedback is the best way to understand the effectiveness of soft skills and can give valuable clues how to recalibrate (if necessary) to achieve the desired outcome. Therefore I encourage coachees to regularly ask for feedback from several sources: from the people impacted by the behaviour and/or actions, observations from various relevant stakeholders and the coachee's own self-reflection (what went well vs. less well).

Learning

We are all largely familiar with soft skills and usually have no issue understanding them intellectually (as opposed to certain technical skills which may require more brainpower to master). Although to truly integrate what is intellectually understood with behaviour and actions, it is important to step back and reflect on the outcomes achieved: results, change and transformation. By doing so the coachee continues to increase their self-awareness, expand their behavioural repertoire and build on the momentum achieved.

About the Comfort Zone

Our comfort zone typically requires little effort from us: it is where we feel at ease. We all have a comfort zone and no two people's comfort zones are exactly the same.

When we choose to leave our comfort zone, we are choosing *courage over comfort*. Because we have previously chosen - or life's circumstances have forced us - to leave our comfort zones at one time or another, these zones are not static: they change over time based on our experiences, insights, skills and actions. We should be mindful that the comfort zone can be a tricky place, as we have a tendency to stay there even when it no longer feels particularly comfortable; and even to the point where it can be downright frustrating to be there. Those feelings of dissatisfaction tell us that it is time to choose courage over comfort and no longer remain in that zone simply because we perceive it to be safe.

Coaching will often require the coachee to step out of their comfort zone to try out new behaviours or new ways of doing things. When working on the action plan part of the coaching process, the coach needs to be cognisant that some actions may be especially challenging for the coachee, necessitating considerable courage on their part. Depending on the coachee's feelings, the coach needs to be prepared to start with smaller, step-by-step actions and increase the challenge as the coachee gains more confidence through their results.

Too old to be coached?

There is a popular and persistent myth that once we reach a certain age change is no longer possible. Although I often hear people state this with certainty, neuroscience now shows this to be untrue. It is absolutely possible to adopt new skills, habits and behaviour *at any age*. Our brain is designed to modify itself to changing situations (also referred to as neuroplasticity) and new pathways are in fact created every day. When we acquire new knowledge and skills, the brain changes itself and creates new neurones, connections and pathways to support that learning. This amazing mechanism is present throughout our lives. The brain learns from repeated experience, and so it is really a matter of motivation, mindset and willingness to learn new skills and adopt new habits and behaviours. This is worth knowing!

"A coach is someone who tells you what you don't want to hear, who has you see what you don't want to see, so you can be who you have always known you could be."

Tom Landry

The Art of Coaching

What makes a Great Coach?

Whether you are a professional coach or an executive employing a coaching leadership style, you need to have a genuine interest in people and a real desire to support them in order to succeed. It is important to understand that the role of a coach is not to stand in the spotlight or try to be clever by persuading the coachee to follow your solutions and advice. Quite the contrary: it is about being a catalyst to enable the coachee to access their knowledge and wisdom. The mission of coaching is about the coachee's journey: encouraging their insights, facilitating their development and honouring their transformation, and taking great pleasure in being of service to that end.

That being the case, curiosity needs to be central to a coach's mindset, and there are three main skills we use to demonstrate our curiosity: presence, listening and asking questions.

Presence

Being fully present with someone is a nonverbal state where we consciously centre all our attention, energy and body language on the other person such that they can register our presence. 'Being in the here and now' is essential to build the rapport and trust required for a successful coaching partnership. It is what enables the coach to create a safe space for the coachee to engage in open conversation and deep reflection.

When starting out as a coach or as a leader/manager developing a coaching leadership style, achieving this state can be challenging as it does not take much for the mind to wander off to other places. In practising present-moment awareness we need to be gentle with ourselves and remember that it is completely normal not to be able to master this skill straightaway; most of us are not used to 'hanging out' in the present moment. But with deliberate intention and a commitment to keep practising, it is encouraging to know that we can make rapid progress.

Being fully present with the coachee and placing trust in the coaching process to unfold (being comfortable with not knowing what will happen next in the coaching conversation) are prerequisites on the road to becoming a great coach. In this way you develop your ability to increasingly coach from your heart and take the conversation to the next level, where transformation occurs.

Listening

Listening is probably the most important yet most neglected communication skill. The saying goes that we have been given two ears and one mouth so we should listen twice as much as we speak, but I think we can safely conclude that this is far from reality!

One of the deepest of human desires is to be understood; we only need to go inside and consider this for a moment to know how true this is. Consequently when someone takes the time to be present and listen with the intention to *really* understand us, our trust, respect and appreciation for that person grows. Yet even though we place such importance on being heard ourselves, most of us tend to forget about this when it comes to extending our listening to others. Isn't this interesting? When listening to others our hearing is often distorted with our own needs, biases and experiences, and so we have a tendency to hear what it means to *us* as opposed to what it really means for the person speaking. By listening poorly we create distance from others, and risk missing information and opportunities that could potentially be useful.

We all recognise the value of 'thinking out loud' with someone where there is no judgement, interruption or advice - just engaged listening. When we are able to speak freely like this, it is amazing how we can connect the dots and quickly gain valuable insights. This occurs because when you speak there are actually *two* people listening: the other person and *you;* and then we may find ourselves spontaneously express: "I can't believe I just thought of that. It's all clear now and I know what to do next!" It is in moments such as these that we experience what is often referred to as the *magic of coaching*.

Thinking about it from this perspective we come to understand just how powerful listening is within the coaching relationship, and that learning to listen well is a worthwhile investment.

Stephen Covey has been instrumental in highlighting the significance of listening to the global business community in his timeless book *The 7 Habits of Highly Effective People*. Covey dedicated an entire habit to listening and coined the expression "Seek first to understand, then to be understood". I love this simple and yet profound statement. To have meaningful coaching sessions the coach needs first to understand the coachee in order to navigate the conversation in a direction that is useful and relevant to them. This is done by listening at the highest level, which I refer to as *open-minded and engaged listening*; although I recently came across another phrase for this which I found quite delightful: *exquisite listening*. Open-minded and engaged (or exquisite) listening necessitates suspending your thoughts, judgements and assumptions - stepping out of your own reality and being fully present - with the aim of entering the other person's reality in order to see things from their point of view.

Being an exquisite listener also means being at ease with silence, and for many of us this can be hard to the point of feeling very uncomfortable. It can be a real challenge to resist the urge to jump in and fill the silence we perceive as awkward. However, to be effective as a coach this is such a crucial skill: just because a coachee is silent, *it does not mean that they are not thinking*. The purpose of the safe space that coaching provides is to allow the coachee both to think out loud and to do quiet internal processing. Once you take your attention off yourself and your discomfort about the silence and simply observe the coachee as they delve deeper into their self-reflection, seeking to connect the dots on their own terms, the results can be truly remarkable. And if you remain in the present moment, you will know when they have finished their internal processing through their verbal or nonverbal communication as they connect back to you.

Why are most of us poor listeners? The answer is simple: we have not been made sufficiently aware about the importance of listening well. But the good news is with this awareness we can practise and become better listeners - starting now!

Questions

Asking relevant and meaningful questions prompts the coachee to tap into their inner wisdom. A keystone in coaching is that people have an abundance of answers within but may not have asked themselves the right questions to access that wisdom. Questions are a powerful means to support coachees to take responsibility for themselves and their situation by approaching, exploring and discovering things from a range of different perspectives.

Questions enable the coachee to gain clarity about their situation, and this in turn leads to ideas, options and ultimately solutions that resonate with them. This is significant because when people are empowered to find the answers for themselves, as opposed to being told what to do, they are far more likely to take ownership and act.

So ask relevant questions and then listen exquisitely.

Much has already been written about how to skilfully construct meaningful questions: how open-ended questions are preferred to closed; how to ask clarifying as opposed to judgemental questions; the power of 'clean' questions, and so on. Therefore, I will not go into any further detail about that here. If you are interested, I have included some of my favourite coaching questions in the appendix.

Coaching as a Profession

Coaching is not the easy or 'light' profession some may initially assume. It requires a deep sense of commitment to the craft, lots of practice and a genuine engagement on the part of the coach. It is wonderfully rewarding to be a positive catalyst in someone's career and life, but it is also hard work to do this well.

Over the years I have interviewed many aspiring coaches who come into the industry with the assumption that coaching is an easy way to make lots of money simply by having conversations, asking some questions and sharing their own valuable experiences. As one hopeful said to me: "I've worked hard in my corporate career and now I want to do something easy for a change. I mean how hard can coaching be?" For someone wanting to deliver a high quality service, produce satisfied clients and build a reputable business, my answer is: "Much more challenging than you think!"

Self-Awareness as a Professional Coach

Coaching is largely about improving performance and achieving goals through self-awareness. Self-awareness is having a conscious understanding of yourself, including your personality, beliefs, values, emotions, behaviours, strengths, weaknesses and motivations. We develop our self-awareness by learning to look at ourselves objectively, relying on facts; by asking for feedback from others; and by engaging in regular self-reflection.

To be a credible catalyst for self-awareness in others, we need to lead by example and work on our own self-awareness by regularly reflecting on ourselves in our role as professional coaches. This fosters our own continuous personal and professional development and will inspire the coachee to do the same.

To Share or Not to Share

It is absolutely central to successful coaching that the coachee feels fully safe and empowered to identify and investigate all of their own thoughts, ideas and options. As coach, this means that you need to refrain from the urge to jump in and provide solutions, even when the best way forward is crystal clear from where you stand. For most novice coaches this can be another testing aspect, in particular if they were expected to give their input in previous professional roles. This was certainly true for me starting out: I frequently had to bite my tongue and learn to place my focus on exquisite listening and asking relevant questions.

There are two schools of thought about sharing input as a coach. One says that the coach should simply refrain from giving any suggestions, full stop. The thinking here is that through questioning and probing, the client will always reach the best solution by exclusively doing their own thinking. The other says that once the client has exhausted their own thoughts, ideas and options and could benefit from some additional perspectives, then the coach can also share their input.

In my experience, I find that when it comes to corporate coaching the second approach makes most sense. If as a coach you have a solid background and extensive experience from the business world, your service to the client would seem incomplete if you did not share from your perspective where this would be appropriate and useful. This can range from brainstorming options to sharing a time when you had a comparable challenge or a similar coachee who felt equally lost or vulnerable in a particular situation. I have found that sharing strengthens the coach-coachee relationship and minimises any risk of the coachee elevating the coach to guru status. Instead we meet as equals, each with our strengths and flaws, doing the best we can. It keeps the partnership *real*.

When I believe I can add something useful to what is being explored, I will often ask permission to share. Doing this emphasises the coach's respect towards the coachee. A simple way to do this is to say: "I have a suggestion/thought/idea - would you like to hear it?"

Remaining Relevant as a Professional Coach

No two people are exactly alike or have precisely the same experience in this world, and this essential human uniqueness is central to coaching. Since we are all different there is no one single coaching approach that will fit everyone; and so coaches need to deliver a highly personalised service to each coachee and their specific situation in a way that brings meaning to them.

Having the ability to tap into a diverse range of skills is therefore crucial for relevance and impact. As professional coaches we need to be cognisant of the need to continuously develop ourselves beyond the basic coaching certification in order to be effective in the service of each unique client. Choose to invest yourself into subjects close to your heart or which spark your keen interest, so that you can be passionate and genuine in your delivery. Some areas where I have chosen to deepen my knowledge are: neuro-linguistic programming, systemic coaching and constellations, neuroscience, emotional intelligence, group mastery, clean language and transpersonal coaching.

Just as with Big Four consultants and lawyers who are regarded as trusted advisors, it is important as a corporate coach to stay up-to-date on latest developments, both within the corporate environment as a whole and in the soft skills topics you coach on. This knowledge is necessary to remain relevant to your clients.

The Importance of Qualification for the Professional Coach

At the time of writing this book, coaching remains a non-regulated profession, meaning that anyone can call themselves a coach. You may be a natural at coaching and have an impressive CV along with credentials such as an MBA, PhD or psychology degree, but it remains my conviction that a recognised certification and accreditation in coaching are essential to deliver the service professionally and credibly. This training gives the coach a solid understanding of what coaching is (and what it is not): its principles, approach, framework, and methodology.

The importance of appropriate and recognised qualifications continues to be highlighted in industry bodies and forums. To put it into obvious context, when the topic comes up I will usually ask: "Would you let someone *without* the relevant qualifications handle your tax returns?" That usually makes people pause for thought. Those posing as professional coaches without the necessary qualifications are not only displaying a certain arrogance, but are also failing to act in the best interest of their clients, and thereby risking tarnishing the reputation of the profession itself.

"The goal of coaching is the goal of good management: to make the most of an organisation's valuable resources"

Harvard Business Review

Coaching and the Corporate World

The Coaching Industry

Coaching is a global multi-billion dollar industry that has continued to grow rapidly for the past several decades - particularly in the corporate arena. Initial scepticism that coaching beyond the sports world would be but a short-lived trend has clearly proved wrong, and its rise is a testament to the significant benefits coaching brings to individuals, teams and organisations.

Corporate coaching is *customised professional development that inspires positive change, improves performance and accelerates growth.* One-to-one coaching (the focus of this book) is predominantly used to encourage and support employees - usually identified talent - to 'raise their game' and make the most of their potential by developing and enhancing their soft skills.

The Corporate/Business World

The world of business has become increasingly complex and bureaucratic. We live in a time where change is constant, competition global; where the pressure to deliver more, faster and better with the fewest possible resources has become the norm; and all this while simultaneously seeking to cultivate the creativity and innovation so desperately needed to remain competitive. In addition, many organisations have adopted intricate matrix structures, with reporting lines across departments and international borders that amplify the complexity and bureaucracy, frequently preventing those organisations from being as flexible and agile as necessary. It is no wonder that some of us will occasionally think back on times when things were simpler with a sense of yearning. And more recently, COVID-19 has brought a whole range of new issues that even the most robust continuity plans did not foresee.

In the face of uncertain and constantly changing business landscapes, finding the right talent is often seen as a priority. In my view, developing and attracting talent is so important that it needs to be high on the CEO and Leadership Team's strategic agenda and have their proactive engagement, rather than Human Resources being solely responsible for it (which is too often the case). It is a fact that the sought-after talent is not always easy to find, hence the now well-established expression 'the war for talent'. Retaining talent has therefore become an increasingly important focus area since the costs associated with recruiting, training and potentially losing that talent are significant.

One of the most effective means of retaining highly skilled and capable people is to give them the opportunity to develop, grow and flourish in their roles. Corporate cultures where professional development in both hard and soft skills is considered a priority have an edge in creating engaged employees. Since an organisation is the product of its people (which too often seems to be forgotten and neglected), ensuring a skilled and equipped workforce is a necessity for companies to survive and thrive. A strategy based on this approach is therefore an absolute win-win for both the organisation and its staff members. Investing in continuous professional development should therefore not be considered a 'nice to have' but a 'need to have'; nor should it be the first thing cut when costs are being reviewed.

Now firmly into the 21st century we have witnessed a global paradigm shift towards principles that are increasingly human by nature and that now more than ever require aptitude from leaders in soft skills. This is not an exhaustive list but rather a summary of points I consider crucial to understand in the context of leadership:

FROM 20th Century	TO 21st Century
• Individual heroic leader • Controlling • Competition • Predictability • Excess focus on profit/greed • Hierarchies • Difference • Winners & losers • Individual contribution • Exclusion	• Develop leaders at all levels • Empowering • Collaboration • Uncertainty • Purpose • Networks • Acceptance • Win-win • Teamwork • Inclusion

In reviewing these points, we see a clear move away from principles and leadership styles steeped in fear and defined by 'Command and Control'. Today's and tomorrow's leaders need to embrace and practise 21st century principles in order to build the human-oriented cultures required to attract and retain talent.

However, most organisations have been slow to acknowledge and adapt to this paradigm shift, thereby increasing the disconnect between themselves and employees' expectations about what life at work should be. This in turn has led to the unprecedented global phenomenon we are witnessing referred to as the 'Great Resignation', which is now forcing business leaders to revisit their company cultures and the way they lead.

About Soft Skills

Soft skills are for the most part easy to understand, which is why we have a tendency to neglect or minimise their importance. However, knowing something intellectually can be very different from integrating it into our conscious mindset and behaviour, and for most of us integrating certain soft skills is not always so straightforward.

We understand that if we want to learn how to play an instrument, speak a new language or perfect our golf swing, we need to make a commitment to learn and then practise over and over to make progress. The same is true if we want to master certain soft skills: we need to be open to learn, to be reflective and to implement new actions/behaviours; to recalibrate when required and practise over and over to become masterful.

In the corporate world, soft skills have historically been viewed as something you either have or you don't - leadership being a good example, with countless debates about whether leaders are 'born' or 'made'. Soft skills have also been viewed largely as something people just need to get on with and learn by themselves. This is why traditionally individuals have been promoted into managerial roles based on their strong technical competencies and with the expectation that they will therefore also be good leaders of people.

It is heartening to note that this is now changing: there is a growing consensus that soft skills, just like technical skills, also need to be learned, developed and sharpened. In many of my client companies, mastering soft skills is steadily becoming a central criterion for career advancement, where at a certain level of seniority technical skills are pretty much seen as baseline and soft skills have become *the difference that makes the difference*.

Coaching is the perfect vehicle to support the development and advancement of these much-needed 21st century soft skills.

Professional Coaching in the Corporate World

Given the distinctiveness and complexity of the corporate world, a solid understanding of this environment on the part of the external coach is key to comprehending the realities that executives face and to be able to empathise with them. Moreover, I believe it is a prerequisite for coaching to be effective and add real value.

PART 2

THE CORPORATE COACHING TOOLKIT

———

"Our deepest fear is not that we are inadequate. Our deepest fear is that we are powerful beyond measure. It is our light, not our darkness, that most frightens us. We ask ourselves, Who am I to be brilliant, gorgeous, talented, fabulous? Actually, who are you not to be?"

Marianne Williamson

———

Introducing the Corporate Coaching Toolkit

The Toolkit is a comprehensive collection of practical, pragmatic and powerful tools that can be used by professional coaches with their clients and by executives to coach themselves.

It is developed drawing on experiences from my own corporate career, invaluable insights from client assignments, coaching-related courses and ongoing research about latest trends and findings in the soft skills and corporate domains; and it is consistently updated and sharpened as trends change and new insights are acquired. Keeping the Toolkit dynamic and up-to-date has been a priority from the outset, so that it is experienced as relevant and meaningful by clients.

The following seven soft skills topics have been included:

1. **Leadership.** Develop as a leader and improve the ability to lead others.

2. **Effective Communication.** Increase awareness about all the elements involved to become an effective communicator.

3. **Emotional Intelligence.** Improve capacity to manage emotions and build good interpersonal relationships.

4. **Stakeholder Management.** Learn to actively manage key internal stakeholders and increase visibility towards them.

5. **Influencing and Negotiation.** Sharpen skills to become more impactful.

6. **Personal Efficiency and Effectiveness.** Develop aptitude in time and priority management to handle business complexity.

7. **Life Balance.** Restore and maintain a balanced life.

Each of these topics comprises an extensive range of elements, perspectives and approaches. It is precisely for this reason that customisation is so important and why each topic needs to be broken down with care to a precise goal formulation that truly resonates with the coachee and their specific situation (see **Inside the Coaching Process** page 25). The Toolkit comes into play once the goal setting part has been completed.

Leadership has continued to be the most popular topic among my clients since the outset of my coaching practice in 2003 and it is the first topic in the Toolkit because it is the most important part in any organisation. Leadership is a substantial and comprehensive area with many facets, which is why this section of the Toolkit is larger than the others.

Every topic begins with an introductory piece to set the scene, and every tool is supplemented with a text box describing the tool and giving guidance on how to use it. The tools have been organised in a kind of chronological order but this should not be regarded as absolute; depending on the coachee and their situation, it may very well make sense to use another order.

Soft skills do overlap and there are several instances of grey areas, for example Leadership, Communication and Emotional Intelligence. Nonetheless, for the sake of focused learning I have found that it makes sense to separate them and address any grey areas as they appear.

The majority of the tools are created by me, with the exception of a few well-known and highly useful models. For topics that are generally less familiar, such as emotional intelligence, the related tools will give more context and tips to the coachee. This provides them with a better comprehension without having to do extensive reading and research on their own. Other tools are templates to encourage the coachee to create their own frameworks, since starting from a blank canvas is not always the best way to promote idea generation and creativity. On the contrary, inspiration often comes from different sources, enabling us to make more creative connections.

As stated in the Introduction, this book has been written with two audiences in mind:

1. For professional coaches working in the corporate/business space wishing to be more effective and impactful in coaching their clients, the tools provide a perfect complement to your coaching conversations and your overall coaching assignments.

2. For executives who prefer to develop their own soft skills unaccompanied and be their own coach. For you, the Toolkit will be of great support to help increase your aptitude, make steady progress and amplify the coaching component of your leadership. Making use of the Toolkit in this context, you naturally become the 'coachee' (recurrently referred to in the tool text-boxes) as you apply the tools on yourself and use them to 'self-coach'.

Clients of mine who are well-seasoned people-managers will sometimes apply certain tools they have used with me to support development of their own direct reports. For those of you interested in this, my recommendation is first to use the tools on yourself so that you understand how they work before trying them with others.

The Value of Individual Reflection

Human beings are creatures of habit and it may not be easy to abandon certain deep-rooted patterns. By the same token, adopting new and better habits can take time to stick. To ensure lasting change I typically recommend one-to-one coaching programmes comprising ten sessions spread over several months. Individual reflection between sessions is invaluable to the success of any coaching programme: it has the potential to bring profound awareness, insights and solutions; and if the coachee writes those insights down, it helps to focus a busy brain on the topic at hand, thereby reinforcing the awareness and learning. For this reason, most of the tools are usually given as 'homework' for coachees to complete by themselves between sessions. Their work is then jointly reviewed and insights discussed as part of the broader coaching conversation.

About Case Studies

Many coaching books include case studies. Because coaching is heavily customised to each individual and their particular situation, and the fact that numerous tools may be used to address different issues around a topic, I have chosen not to use case studies but instead have provided a text box for each tool. These text boxes contain a description of the tool and guidance on how to use it.

Use the Tools Mindfully - a Note to the Professional Coach

Not all the tools under a soft skills topic will be relevant to every coachee, so you will need to pick and choose wisely. It is about adopting a 'person-and-situation-based' approach, where you consider the unique circumstances of each individual coachee to assess what tools are the best match.

Remember, your coaching skills are principal to the process and the tools a *complement* to the coaching conversation - take care not to let the tools take over your ability to coach effectively. There may be coaching sessions where the best way forward is without using any tools, so select them only where appropriate and when they add value, with the intention of making each person's coaching journey a meaningful and rich experience.

Leadership

"Leadership and learning are indispensable to each other."

John F. Kennedy

About Leadership

Good leadership is critical to cultivate a high-performing work environment. Most of us know from direct experience that the difference between an engaged and a disengaged workforce often stems from the quality of its leadership.

One of the most common questions among executives is: *What does it take to become a great leader?*

We all recognise great leaders in our presence, but interestingly no leader seems to adhere to a single template. As with soft skills in general, what works for one leader may not work for another. The topic of leadership is big and multi-faceted and triggers a wide range of thoughts and opinions about how to encapsulate it. A myriad of books and articles are published every year which are geared towards executives in pursuit of the magic formula... and yet there is no consensus about the precise definition of leadership.

Something most people do seem to agree on, however, is that leadership is no longer only about seniority and position: it is more about how you behave and what you do. So someone may be in a top leadership position but not be actively leading - something we quite often witness in business and politics. And leaders can exist in all levels of an organisation without having a formal managerial title. As Henry Ford once said: "You don't have to hold a position in order to be a leader."

Leadership is not static: what is required of a leader evolves over time. The road to building future-proof organisations is no longer through 'control and command' leadership steeped in fear, but rather via leaders who are able to inspire trust and share a clear, meaningful vision with those they lead. Leaders who take care to listen and create inclusive, respectful and fair learning environments that are psychologically safe, enabling people to perform at their natural best. Leaders who not only achieve success for themselves, but who also take care to make a positive difference for others. It is sometimes said that the best leaders are those who lead not just with their head but their heart too - *when feeling and thought meet,* as Daniel Goleman so beautifully puts it.

For a corporate vision to be captivating it needs to touch people's hearts in a way that feels meaningful and relevant to them. Far too often leaders tend to forget that it is the *people* who will execute the strategic plan: it is their work that will determine the results, not the strategic plan itself. In coaching sessions I will often draw attention to this by reminding my most senior clients: "Who are you without your people?"

Leadership is a contagious, emotional transaction: whether leaders are aware of it or not, their employees are watching and are emotionally affected by them. Leaders' styles, behaviours, moods and actions produce considerable ripples throughout an organisation; the tone and culture are set at the top of the house. When employees trust and are inspired by their leaders, they will engage in the workplace and achieve remarkable things.

Even though there is no consensus on the exact definition of leadership, I find it useful to have one as a point of reference. My preferred definition (to date) is by McKinsey experts Claudio Feser, Michael Rennie and Nicolai Nielsen. They define leadership as: *a set of behaviours that leaders exercise to influence organisational members to achieve a higher alignment on the direction that the organisation is taking, to achieve a better execution of the strategy, and for the organisation to continuously renew itself.*[4]

---

4 Leadership At Scale: Better leadership, better results, 2019

This definition resonates with me because unlike many others it underscores the comprehensive range effective leadership needs to cover in the corporate domain. It highlights how leadership is contextual and invites leaders to step back and ask themselves: Given our organisation, our people, our culture, our vision and the environment in which we operate, *what is required from me as leader (and us, as the leadership team)?*

To develop and improve leadership skills requires commitment and the willingness to sometimes be vulnerable in the process. Research professor Brené Brown describes vulnerability as having the courage to show up when you can't predict or control the outcome[5]; and as we try out new leadership behaviours we may find that we need to tap into that courage. Working on our leadership requires us to have an open mind in order to self-reflect on our strengths and weaknesses; to explore, learn and adopt new behaviours.

These days we know that leaders need to *inspire* rather than *force* people to follow them. To achieve this they need to be relevant to those they lead, but what does that mean and how does one go about being inspiring to others? This is something that everyone needs to explore for themselves in light of their own situation, personality, talents, skills and experience - and to bring this out in a way that feels honest and authentic.

As a first step on this journey it is important to understand what is required from the current role (the mandate), what the leader is seeking to achieve in the role (the purpose), and whether their current leadership style supports them in this mission. By engaging in introspection to increase self-awareness, gain clarity about gaps and practise new behaviours consistently, they can acquire new competencies that expand their leadership repertoire.

Because the requirements of leadership evolve, leaders need to remain open and agile. COVID-19 brought a new range of leadership considerations where many of my client leaders, naturally completely caught off guard at the time of confinement, were asking: *How do I meet this new leadership challenge? What is required from me now? How do I show up authentically? How do I communicate effectively during this crisis to strike the right balance between empathy and direction? What decisions need to be made to ensure the safety of our people? What leadership qualities do I need to develop or bring out in myself?*

The effects of the pandemic and the overall rapid pace of change that has become part of the business world will continue to impact what is expected from leadership going forward. Leadership agility has become more important than ever before.

Having conversations about leadership is clearly easier than actually leading; great leadership takes work, time and energy. And since followers are smart, actions behind the words are required to establish trust and engagement. These days you can be the smartest person in the organisation, but if no one wants to follow you, you cannot be a leader. You will walk alone and your people will be disengaged. Benjamin Hooks expresses this most eloquently when he says:

"If you think you are leading and turn around to see no one following, then you are just taking a walk."

---

5   *The Call to Courage* Netflix special by Brené Brown

"Leadership is a choice. Every single one of us can make the choice to be the leader we wish we had."

Simon Sinek

1.1 What Makes a Good Leader?

Leadership

Please insert your answers directly under each question:

1. What does leadership mean to you?

_____

_____

_____

Think of one or more people in a leadership position (past or present) who have inspired you and whom you would be willing to follow:

2. List the _qualities_ (key words) of that leader(s) you find inspiring.

_____

_____

_____

3. To be a good leader, what _values_ do you believe someone needs to have?
(Values are a person's principles and standards about what is important.)
List the values.

_____

_____

_____

4. In your opinion what specific _behaviours_ should a good leader demonstrate when interacting and relating to others?
List the behaviours.

_____

_____

_____

5. Now go back and review your answers. What comes to your mind now you have completed the exercise?

_____

_____

_____

About Tool 1.1 What Makes a Good Leader?

Even though leadership is a hot topic, people seldom stop to think about what it means to them in any profound way, which is why I usually begin with this tool in the Leadership Toolkit. The first question, "What does leadership mean to you?" is an important starting point on the journey of leadership development, and often has coachees spending more time than they initially expected to clearly articulate this for themselves.

Turning the coachee's attention outward to think about leader role models and their own experiences of being led brings to the surface the qualities they have appreciated and found inspiring. This is a good way to activate the emotive aspect, which is essential for effective leadership (as opposed to coming at things from a purely intellectual point of view), and to think about the values and behaviours the coachee considers important in a leadership context.

It can be very helpful to identify and observe role models who possess qualities that inspire us and to get curious about the strategies they apply to be effective. However, we need to be mindful that when it comes to soft skills there is no simple copy-paste. Once we have observed and studied others, we then need to find strategies to bring out those desired qualities in ways that feel right to us, so that we can be true to who we are and come across as genuine to others.

Someone once told me that the things that inspire us are in fact a reflection of traits we ourselves possess; and that these traits may be active or dormant but they do reside within us. I remember being intrigued by this remark, thinking to myself: If this is true, then with increased self-awareness these qualities are accessible to us and with practice can be consciously integrated into our mindset and behaviour. My work with coachees has provided a perfect testing ground for this assumption, where I have indeed found that greater clarity about what we consider to be important and inspiring often triggers our motivation to gravitate towards those things and seek to bring them out and/or strengthen them.

How to use the tool

As part of your initial conversation about leadership (preferably towards the end), take the coachee through the tool so that it is clear what you expect from them in terms of completing it. Give it to them as homework so that they continue to think about the topic by themselves and then together with you in the following session.

Sometimes a coachee will tell you that they cannot think of a single person during the course of their professional life who they consider to be a good leader. If this is the case I will ask them to think about anyone in a leadership position, and this usually results in them choosing someone famous whom they admire.

It is also worth noting that some people have extremely high (to the point of unreasonable) expectations of their leaders and find it hard to accept or forgive any character flaw, but rather expect leaders to be some kind of super-humans. When encouraged to explore this belief with the coach, they usually realise that this is unrealistic and may even be counter-productive to their own leadership development. Therefore when presenting this tool I find it helpful to frame the exercise with the acknowledgement that no-one is perfect: that as human beings we are all flawed, and that the purpose of this exercise is not about finding a perfect person, but rather thinking about someone in a leadership position who has inspired us to follow them and considering why.

Not surprisingly, when coachees are invited to think about what makes a leader inspiring most of the qualities identified will be in the soft skills domain. Their reflections and insights provide a good foundation for further exploration.

"Knowing yourself is the beginning of all wisdom."

Aristotle

1.2 Self-Awareness

Leadership

Insert your answers directly under each question:

1. **When do you take time to reflect about yourself in your role as leader?**

   _____

   _____

2. **How would you describe your leadership style?** (List your strong and weak points)

   _____

   _____

3. **How aware are you about the impact you have on others (as leader), and is your impact what you want it to be?** (Please explain)

   _____

   _____

4. **What precisely do you want to achieve for the area of business you manage?**
   (List your vision/purpose)

   _____

   _____

5. **How would you describe your leadership voice and how would you like to continue to develop it?**

   _____

   _____

6. **Knowing that today's leaders need to inspire followers:**

   – **What leadership behaviours do you need to demonstrate and/or develop to be effective?**

   _____

   – **What behaviours are you displaying that prevent you from achieving this?**

   _____

7. **What kind of leader do you want to be?**
   (What do you want to be known for (legacy)? How do you want others to speak about you?)

   _"I want to be the kind of leader who _____"_ (complete the sentence)

8. **How will you know that you are succeeding in your practice to become the leader you want to be? What will the success factors/evidence be?** (Please elaborate on your answer)

   _____

   _____

About Tool 1.2 Self-Awareness

Once the coachee has spent time thinking about leadership, their experiences being led by others and what they consider to be important in terms of leadership values and behaviour in **Tool 1.1**, it is time to turn the thinking inward - to reflect on themselves and their own leadership.

Self-awareness is knowing ourselves and our impact on others. It is one of the most critical qualities of good and effective leadership, and helps to keep us focused and grounded. Whether you are an aspiring manager or an experienced executive, taking time on a regular basis to reflect on and hone your skills is an essential aspect on the path to inspirational leadership.

How to use the tool

At a suitable moment in the coaching conversation, take the coachee through the questions in the tool. Set context and expectations and ask them to complete it for the next session.

To note:

Question 3 is closely linked to emotional intelligence and requires the coachee to consider their leadership from the perspective of others. Taking this external perspective is often new to coachees and will typically trigger their curiosity to start paying attention to and understanding this aspect better.

Question 4 may look easy at first glance, but to articulate one's vision/purpose in a way that is understood and compelling to others often requires some in-depth thinking. Having a captivating vision is necessary to create engagement. Only when we are clear about it can we communicate it in such a way that inspires others and creates buy-in, support and alignment.

Question 5 is often particularly challenging. To help spark thinking it is good to frame the coachee's leadership voice. Framing can go something like this: *Your leadership voice is a reflection of how you show up as a leader. It is a powerful tool that conveys your core values in your interactions with others, for example how you articulate your vision/purpose, contribute your ideas, engage and inspire others, deliver feedback or handle conflict.*

Finding or developing one's leadership voice may require some courage at the outset, so starting with smaller actions to practise in 'safe' situations and building from there is usually a good approach to build the coachee's confidence.

Question 6 is a reminder that today's leaders need to inspire followers. It encourages the coachee to think about what this means for them and what they would need to pay attention to or develop further, so that they may authentically bring this out in themselves.

Overall coachees will find this tool notably more challenging to complete than **Tool 1.1** because most will not have reflected on these types of questions about themselves and their leadership. Completion of the exercise usually takes the coaching conversation to a place where real transformation can begin.

"Who you are, what your values are, what you stand for... They are your anchor, your north star. You won't find them in a book. You'll find them in your soul"

Anne M. Mulcahy

1.3 What do you Value?

Leadership

In a leadership role, having clarity about one's core personal values is a critical part of self-awareness. Our effectiveness in 'living our values' will be reflected in our leadership voice and personal brand (how we are perceived by the people around us).

A values-based leadership is about consciously accessing our inner compass when we *set goals, communicate, influence, make decisions and lead others:* it enables us to act authentically and create the trust of others.

Please reflect on the following questions and insert your answers under each question:

1. What are 4 personal values you want to be known for, as part of your personal brand as leader?

_____

_____

_____

_____

2. How are the values you have selected important to you?
   (Please answer for each respective value)

_____

_____

_____

_____

3. How will you go about 'being' and 'living' your selected values in a way that is visible to others?

_____

_____

_____

_____

4. How will you remind yourself and hold yourself accountable?

_____

_____

_____

_____

About Tool 1.3 What do you Value?

Our values are our fundamental principles and standards about what is important. They are an integral part of what motivates us and drives our behaviour. When coachees are asked to articulate their values, they are reminded about what is truly meaningful to them. As the first sentence in this tool states, *clarity about one's core personal values is a critical part of a leader's self-awareness.* Having this clarity helps to assess whether behaviour, decisions, actions and leadership are *congruent* with the values. (Some values can at times be difficult to live up to due to distractions, challenging situations or simply forgetfulness.)

This tool continues to build on the work completed in **Tool 1.1 What Makes a Good Leader?** where coachees were asked to think about values and behaviour in a larger leadership context. Here focus is placed on their *own* values that they want to proactively integrate into their personal brand, and how they will go about doing this so that it is visible to others.

How to use the tool

It can be useful to set the context around values in relation to leadership as this is not always obvious to everyone.

In the coaching conversation following the coachee's completion of the tool, I address the aspect of congruence of values in relation to behaviour, decisions and actions. I encourage the coachee to reflect about when there is congruence, when this may be more of a challenge and why that is so.

When it comes to accountability I may also ask if the coachee has someone in their close professional circle whom they could ask to help hold them accountable.

Keeping a daily to-do list for tasks and priorities is well established and I was delighted to come across the idea of doing the same with values: to take a few minutes each day and create an intention around how we want to show up, and then complement our to-do list with a 'to-be' list. The idea is that while preparing and thinking about what will be important that day, we select one or two values to have at the forefront of our minds. The to-be list should be kept close (ideally be part of the to-do list) throughout the day as a reminder. Coachees who are enthusiastic about this idea often report back how much more focused this has made them on the values important to them, as well as the positive effects they are experiencing.

———————

"The best leaders don't know just one style of Leadership - they're skilled at several, and have the flexibility to switch between styles as the circumstances dictate."

Daniel Goleman

———————

1.4 Six Leadership Styles

Leadership

Since leadership is the most popular soft skills topic among executives, it is no surprise that a significant amount of research has been conducted about it. By interviewing close to 4,000 managers, six distinct leadership styles have been uncovered[6]:

Insight into the Six Leadership Styles

	Visionary	Pacesetting	Affiliate	Coercive	Democratic	Coaching
Leader's modus operandi	Mobilises and inspires people towards a shared vision - larger purpose	Sets high standards and expectations for excellence	Creates harmony and builds emotional bonds between people	Demands immediate compliance	Values people's input and gets commitment through participation	Empowers and develops people for the future
In a phrase	"Come with me"	"Do as I do, now"	"People come first"	"Do what I tell you"	"What do you think?"	"What would You propose the next step to be?"
Style works best when...	When explicit vision and direction is required	To get high-quality and quick results	To heal conflicts, motivate in stressful times and strengthen connections	In a crisis, or to kickstart a change, or with problem staff	To build buy-in, consensus or get valuable input	Improve performance by building long-term capabilities and cultivate ownership
Long-term impact on culture	+	−	+	−	+	+

Think further about how the different leadership styles relate to you, what you are seeking to achieve in your role and answer these questions in a separate note:

1. **Which of the six is/are your preferred/natural style?**

_____

_____

2. **Which of the six would be useful to incorporate into your main leadership style/s and to what end?**

_____

_____

3. **What do you need to do to make this happen in order to expand your leadership repertoire and thereby become more effective in your leadership role?**

_____

_____

---

6 Hay/McBer and Daniel Goleman

About Tool 1.4 Six Leadership Styles

It is not uncommon for people to think about things in terms of 'black and white' and 'either/or', and this is also true when thinking about leadership styles. We tend to view leaders as either authoritarian or humane, whereas in reality there are more than two directly opposing styles. Different situations, people and challenges will require a different leadership approach. Flexibility in behaviour and/or style depending on the situation is sometimes referred to as *situational leadership*.

When coaching for leadership development, having a model reference point that describes different styles is most useful for the conversation. A good model will provide the coachee with a framework that prompts quick detection of where strengths and weaknesses lie and link these back to their work reality.

Many models have been developed around leadership styles. One that continues to stand out for me is Daniel Goleman's work based on research by consulting firm Hay/McBer. By studying close to 4,000 managers they uncovered six distinct leadership styles, and were also able to determine each style's long-term effect on corporate culture, which in turn has a proven direct impact on financial performance and profitability. The latter perspective highlights the significant role that leadership plays and helps to fuel the coachee's motivation to develop their skills. Of the six styles, Visionary, Affiliate, Democratic and Coaching generate conditions that promote engagement and performance. The other two, Pacesetting and Coercive, are useful in certain situations but should be applied with care due to their potentially negative long-term impact in the workplace.

The model demonstrates in a simple and elegant way why no one leadership style can be regarded as absolute; how no one style fits all. Quite the contrary, it underscores that to be an effective leader one needs to be mindful about what the person or situation requires and use the style most suitable for it. Because of its clarity and simplicity, this model provides a great reference for exploration and I will often return to it during the course of the leadership conversation.

How to use the tool

Coachees usually have an idea about what they want to accomplish and/or develop when it comes to their leadership, but may feel a bit stuck in taking the first steps from intention to action. The feeling of "Where do I begin?" is normal and is where the action part of the coaching process becomes beneficial to the coachee.

This tool will usually spark great interest and engagement on the part of the coachee because it provides the kind of framework many have yearned for: it makes the abstract more real and concrete.

I will typically take the coachee through the styles using the first diagram, Six Leadership Styles at a Glance*, and give a short background in line with the description above (About the Tool). I then move to the more detailed chart and ask questions that help the coachee relate back to their role and mission. Once the coachee has formulated an initial analysis with me, they will be asked to continue their reflection and answer the three questions on leadership style as homework.

Even though the majority of coachees are enthusiastic about this tool, for some this exercise can be initially daunting. They may feel overwhelmed at the prospect of developing some of these styles and so it is important to be gentle, understanding and encouraging. However, in my experience the sense of overwhelm tends to dissolve rather quickly once coachees start to turn their insights into meaningful actions, when they can witness positive results and feel how they are growing both personally and professionally.

* I have exchanged one phrase in the Coaching Leadership Style from the original "Try this" to "What would you propose the next step to be?" as I think it better reflects a coaching approach that encourages empowerment and taking ownership.

"Leadership, like swimming, cannot be learned by reading about it."

Henry Mintzberg

1.5 Self-Reflection

Leadership

Please insert your answers directly under each question:

1. **Are my (leadership) decisions and actions resulting in the outcomes I want?**
   (If yes, then what is the evidence of that? If no, then why not?)

   _____

   _____

   _____

2. **How well do I connect, listen and seek to understand the people around me?**
   (Please elaborate)

   _____

   _____

   _____

3. **If I put myself in the shoes of those I lead, does my style and behaviour reflect how _I_ want to be led - in other words, would I follow me?**
   (Please elaborate)

   _____

   _____

   _____

4. **Am I leading and communicating sufficiently from a bigger picture perspective (vision, purpose and strategy)? If not, then what is blocking me from doing so?**
   (If distraction is an issue, then what specifically is distracting me?)

   _____

   _____

   _____

5. **How often do I seek feedback about myself from those around me?**

   _____

   _____

   _____

6. **Am I taking care of myself and my wellbeing to be the best possible version of myself?**
   (Is anything missing/what do I need?)

   _____

   _____

   _____

7. Am I in alignment with the kind of leader I want to be?
(Refer back to your answer to question 8 in Tool 2.1 Self-Awareness)

_____

_____

_____

8. Following my reflections, what do I need to be more mindful about?

_____

_____

_____

About Tool 1.5 Self-Reflection

Regular self-reflection is required to cultivate and maintain a good degree of self-awareness. I recommend that executives block some time (ideally weekly) to contemplate how they lead and how impactful they are. Greater self-awareness helps to adjust ineffective behaviours and styles and therefore to make better decisions.

However, blocking time is the easy part; how to reflect on oneself is not always as simple. This tool provides examples of questions to guide this kind of reflection, and aims to motivate the coachee to create the habit of doing this regularly.

How to use the tool

By the time I introduce this tool to a coachee, we have had a number of in-depth coaching conversations about leadership in relation to their role. They will have tried out some new styles and ways of approaching things and implemented a number of actions both for themselves and for the people they lead. This exercise gives them the opportunity to think about their leadership effectiveness and to address issues around this in the coaching process.

"You cannot be everything to everyone. If you decide to go north, you cannot go south at the same time."

Jeroen De Flander

1.6 Role Clarification

Leadership

Please complete the following exercise:

- List all your work-related tasks under each of the 3 categories below and *be specific*.
- Include tasks that you may not be doing currently (for whatever reason) but that are part of your role and put those in another colour.
- Remember to include your yearly objectives.
- Insert the **current** and **desired** big-line percentages (%) of your time spent in each of the 3 categories: Strategy, Leadership and Execution/Operational.

Strategy (What are the strategic elements/requirements of your role? The 'Big Picture')	*Current time* _____ %	*Desired time* _____ %

Leadership	*Current time* _____ %	*Desired time* _____ %

Execution / Operational	*Current time* _____ %	*Desired time* _____ %

Time to reflect:
Please insert your answers directly under each question below. As you think deeper about this, you may want to go back and review your work in the categories above to ensure you have included all the tasks.

1. **What is expected from you in your role?**
   (Describe in a few concise sentences the things you are measured on)

2. **Thinking about what is expected from you, what are your top priorities?**

3. **Are you spending sufficient time working on the things that will enable you to achieve what is expected from you?** (your mandate)

_____

_____

4. **If not, then what is distracting you?**

_____

_____

5. **What is required from you from a _leadership_ perspective?**

_____

_____

6. **What specifically are you doing in the _strategy_ element of your role to align with the company's overall strategy?**

_____

_____

7. **What is the bigger picture here - what has become clear to you?**

_____

_____

8. **How will you get from 'current time' to 'desired time'?**

_____

_____

About Tool 1.6 Role Clarification

Many executives can identify with the feeling of being busy all the time at work, but at the end of the working day still feeling like they did not accomplish much. When we feel this way it is usually because we are not spending sufficient time focusing and working on the right things - the priorities of our role. Corporate life is complex: there is a lot to manage and it is easy to get distracted and dragged into details. As a result we can feel overwhelmed or that we are not operating at our best.

This tool brings clarity to all the tasks that make up the coachee's time ('current time'). Only by fully understanding what is currently going on does it make sense to think about how to improve the balance ('desired time') and to explore potential actions to achieve this. I see an executive's role composed of three main parts: Strategy, Leadership and Execution/Operational. Viewing things from this perspective allows coachees to understand where they are falling short and what would be required to align the work to their role.

How to use the tool

I will ask coachees to complete this exercise when it becomes apparent during the coaching conversation that the coachee:

- Has an overriding feeling of overwhelm and lack of control over their situation.
- Is working on comfort zone tasks that are no longer part of their role.
- Is not spending sufficient time on strategic and/or leadership elements required by their role.

>>

In the first part of the tool, coachees are requested to fill out all the work-related tasks in each of the 3 categories and to be exhaustive, so that we can get a complete picture of their current reality. They are also requested to include tasks that they *should* be doing as part of their role but (for whatever reason) are not.

In the second part of the tool, the questions help to bring the priorities of their role to the surface and to clearly articulate the leadership and strategic expectations.

As a result of this exercise most coachees realise they are spending far too much time in Execution/Operational and not nearly enough in Strategy and Leadership. To complement this insight I will often use **Tool 6.1 Eisenhower Matrix**, as it gives an additional very useful perspective into the coachee's current way of working. The exercise often also reveals that many people are not comfortable in the strategic domain and may even be unsure about what those elements of their role are. This clarity is important for the coaching to deal with the correct issues.

This tool is dynamic and is used to track the coachee's progress as actions are implemented to move towards their desired situation. If a significant shift is required, then I will ask them to define milestones for a step-by-step move from 'here' to 'there'.

"Strategy is a fancy word for coming up with a long-term plan and putting it into action."

Ellie Pidot

1.7 Strategic Thinking

Leadership

Strategic thinking is largely about proactively challenging the status quo from a bigger picture perspective. Thoughtfully crafted questions are indispensable to access useful insights and stimulate creativity.

Below are some examples of questions that encourage strategic thinking. Use them to fuel your ability to formulate questions relevant to your business and feel free to use the ones that resonate.

- ✓ *In our day-to-day activities, where are we spending the majority of our time?*
- ✓ *Is our current way of operating in line with the priorities set out in our strategy? Are we on target? Are there any gaps? What are they and how do we close them?*
- ✓ *How would we rate our overall efficiency? Where are we getting distracted and/or wasting time?*
- ✓ *What have we learned since our last strategic checkpoint (for example about clients, services/products, markets, trends) that we need to consider moving forward?*
- ✓ *How do we know we are bringing the value our clients are looking for? What is the concrete evidence for this? What do we need to learn more about and where can we improve?*
- ✓ *What is our edge and are we playing to it?*
- ✓ *Are we fully exploiting identified opportunities?*
- ✓ *Does our culture promote, recognise and value creative and innovative thinking? If yes, how so? If no, what is missing in order to improve?*
- ✓ *Are we capitalising sufficiently on our diversity (by means of inclusiveness) in order to be as creative and innovative as we could be?*
- ✓ *Is our strategy and vision clearly understood by our employees?*
- ✓ *How well are we doing in our target market and vis-à-vis our competition? Are we on track?*

By creating regular opportunities for ourselves and our team(s) to pause and engage on these types of questions, we can rapidly develop our capacity to think strategically and cascade this important skill. Being inclusive in this way engages and motivates employees to be part of shaping the agenda. It provides a platform where we learn from one another and ensures that we continuously 'sharpen the saw' by drawing on diverse experiences, opinions and ideas.

Please reflect and answer these questions in a separate note:

1. How frequently would it be beneficial (to be effective in your role) to block regular time for strategic thinking?

---

2. What would be examples of useful questions specific to your area of responsibility?

About Tool 1.7 Strategic Thinking

As executives take on senior roles there is an expectation that they also become more strategic - and rightly so. Engaging in regular strategic thinking and having a solid plan that covers all aspects impacting the business (and is fully aligned with the overall vision) is crucial to successfully lead transformational change and ensure the organisation's long-term sustainability.

However, becoming 'more strategic' is an abstract concept often seen as complex and therefore difficult to grasp. Making the shift requires most people to step out of their comfort zone where they execute well on tangible tasks (which has resulted in their promotion) into this more ambiguous zone that requires dealing with the 'bigger picture' aspects. In this transition, many struggle to understand where to begin or even to ask for support, because they believe that everyone should be able to succeed naturally on their own. This is an interesting myth since reality shows that the majority of executives struggle and are falling short in this part of their roles. One study in 2015 of 6,000 senior executives showed that only 8% of the respondents turned out to be strategic leaders.[7]

Engaging in strategic thinking is key to stay on top of the universal issues that impact the organisation (and/or part of the business), as well as ensuring continuous buy-in and motivation among employees to pull in the same direction. To do this it is necessary to pause and reflect about how we are operating on a daily basis and where we are placing our attention, and to verify if we are indeed achieving the results we want. We can do this thinking by ourselves in our reflective time and we can also do this with our team(s). For best possible outcomes I recommend doing both.

Approaching things from this standpoint moves us away from a mindset of ambiguous complexity to one that is practical and pragmatic. This tool was developed to help de-mystify strategic thinking and motivate coachees to set time aside for it.

How to use the tool

Coachees who benefit from this tool are either struggling with or are keen to improve their skills in this area.

Once these types of questions become part of the coachee's reflective time individually and together with their team(s), they will often experience a sense of relief and pride in themselves as they experience positive traction in this area. Fresh insights and conclusions will open the door to new opportunities. Those who conduct strategic sessions with their teams frequently report back that these sessions contribute positively to the overall team spirit - because being involved in brainstorming and decision-making that influences their work makes people *feel* valued.

---

7   The hidden talent: Ten ways to identify and retain transformational leaders, 2015, PwC

Real leadership is not about prestige, power or status. It's about responsibility."

Robert Joss

1.8 Leader Qualities

Leadership

Below is a compilation of essential leadership qualities.
How would you rate yourself on a scale from 1-5 for these qualities (5 being highest) and why?

Your Approach

1. I take time on a regular basis to **reflect** on my behaviour and actions and my impact on those around me. (Self-awareness)

   Rating: _____

   Reason: _____

2. I have a clear **vision (purpose)** and **strategy** for my area and I communicate these regularly to those who need to be aware.

   Rating: _____

   Reason: _____

3. I take time for **strategic thinking** (to consider the bigger picture, overall trends, new information, long-term perspective and planning, to seek to 'connect the dots').

   Rating: _____

   Reason: _____

4. I seek to **lead by example** by role modelling my own and the company values and displaying a positive, professional attitude.

   Rating: _____

   Reason: _____

5. I **accept responsibility** for positive results.

   Rating: _____

   Reason: _____

6. I **accept responsibility** for negative results.

   Rating: _____

   Reason: _____

7. I am **open** and **clear** in my communication (and expectations).

   Rating: _____

   Reason: _____

8. I am **consistent** in my communication and actions.

   Rating: _____

   Reason: _____

9. I gravitate towards **humility** (as opposed to arrogance).

    Rating: _____

    Reason: _____

10. I have **courage** to confront **challenging situations** and **conflicts**.

    Rating: _____

    Reason: _____

11. I make the necessary **difficult decisions** and take the time to explain the rationale behind them.

    Rating: _____

    Reason: _____

12. I cultivate **strong professional relationships** at all relevant levels. (Stakeholder management)

    Rating: _____

    Reason: _____

13. I ensure that I continuously engage in **self-development** and build my **business expertise**.

    Rating: _____

    Reason: _____

Leading Others

14. I am **available** for the people I lead and make sure they feel **supported**.

    Rating: _____

    Reason: _____

15. I take care to **listen** with the intention to understand.

    Rating: _____

    Reason: _____

16. I am mindful to embrace **diversity** and to be **inclusive** and this is also reflected when I recruit**.**

    Rating: _____

    Reason: _____

17. I take care to extend, build and maintain **trust** with others.

    Rating: _____

    Reason: _____

18. I demonstrate **empathy** for others when required and show that I care.

    Rating: _____

    Reason: _____

19. I use authority in a balanced way and seek primarily to **inspire action**. (Situational Leadership)

    Rating: _____

    Reason: _____

20. I achieve results by **effective delegation** so that I can sufficiently focus on the leadership and strategic aspects of my role.

Rating: _____

Reason: _____

21. I actively **develop, coach** and **empower** my team members to be responsible for their own commitments, decisions and actions.

Rating: _____

Reason: _____

22. I encourage **collaboration** on strategies and setting meaningful goals.

Rating: _____

Reason: _____

23. I encourage **strategic** and **creative thinking** and challenging of the status quo.

Rating: _____

Reason: _____

24. I seek to **guide, question** and **challenge** (as opposed to simply telling or giving the answers).

Rating: _____

Reason: _____

25. I **recognise** and **acknowledge** the achievements of others (praise) to motivate and make them feel valued.

Rating: _____

Reason: _____

26. I give honest and specific **negative feedback** when required and in a timely manner so that my team members can continue to grow and develop.

Rating: _____

Reason: _____

27. I recognise that **different people** may need **a different type of leading/coaching.**
(Situational leadership)

Rating: _____

Reason: _____

Reflection Point:
What are your conclusions after completing this exercise?

_____

_____

_____

_____

About Tool 1.8 Leader Qualities

As leadership is a comprehensive topic with so many facets, it can be useful to break them down into distinct qualities and let coachees rate themselves against those qualities. This enables them to assess their current status and overall progress. What makes this exercise valuable is that each rating needs to be supported with an explanation. It compels the coachee to really think about each quality from a broader perspective and promotes continuous self-awareness.

How to use the tool

Once a coachee feels they have made good progress in their leadership development, I show them this set of leader qualities and ask them if they would like to go through and complete the exercise.

I usually go through the first few qualities together with the coachee, especially probing the reason - the 'why' part - and encourage them to think about each element from different viewpoints. Where the coachee is unsure about how to rate themselves, I may encourage them to find out how they are doing by asking trusted colleagues for feedback - which is ultimately the best way to really understand the impact of our soft skills.

In the session that follows we review their answers and discuss their insights together. By completing this exercise, most coachees realise the importance of taking time to think and reflect on their leadership with more regularity, as well as actually implementing and practising certain qualities. If relevant, I draw attention to the 'to-be' list described in the text box from **Tool 1.3 What do you value?** to create an intention around what leadership qualities/behaviours to practise on a daily basis.

"Great things in business are never done by one person; they're done by a team of people."

Steve Jobs

1.9 Leading the Team

Leadership

Please reflect and answer the questions below:

1. **In an average week, how much of your time (%) do you spend with your team?** (To support, guide, coach, develop and mentor them)

2. **Is the team aligned and working in the same direction towards a common overall vision?**

3. **If asked, would your team members be able to paraphrase your vision/purpose for the area of business you are responsible for?**

4. **How do you think you are perceived by your team as their leader?**

5. **Is it aligned with how you want to be perceived by them?** (If not, then what is the gap?)

6. **What do the individual team members need and want from you?**
   (Are you sure you know?)

7. **Are you able to provide that support and would you say that you are consistent in your service to them?** (Please explain)

8. **How are efforts and accomplishments recognised?**

9. **Describe the level of openness between you and your team members.**
   (Do they speak openly about the things you need to know, when they have made a mistake, their worries and concerns, their professional ambitions, etc.)

10. **How do you go about building trust between you and the team?**

11. **How would you describe the level of inclusion in the team? In what circumstances would there be room for improvement?** (Please elaborate)

12. **How do team members connect, team and collaborate together? What works well and where is there room for improvement?**
(Is it 'everyone for themselves' or will team members actively offer support to each other? Are there common team goals?)

13. **Do you involve your team in the more strategic aspects of your role/work?**
(If yes, how do you do this and what is your experience? If no, are there areas where there could be value in doing this?)

14. **How would you describe the overall level of engagement in the team and is it where you want it to be?**

15. **What are you doing to create an environment that is psychological safe, enabling your team members to perform at their natural best?** (Please elaborate)

Having completed this exercise, go back and review your conclusions and then answer the question below.

16. **As leader of your team, what do you want to:**

• *Continue doing?*

• *Start doing?*

• *Stop doing?*

About Tool 1.9 Leading the Team

When coaching is focused on team leadership, one of the first things I ask for is an organisation chart. This is helpful for the coach to understand how the team is structured, where it is positioned in relation to the other departments and how reporting lines are organised.

This tool is a good starting point for the coachee to consider a range of aspects related to leading their team.

How to use the tool

The coachee's answers to the questions in this tool will reveal which areas will benefit from specific attention in the coaching. Particularly thought-provoking questions are 4, 6, 10, 11, 13 and 15.

>>

To note:

Question 11 encourages thinking about the level of inclusion in the team. We are inclusive when everyone in the team is respected and treated fairly, when we are open to working together and to considering each person's perspective and contribution. Even though companies may be diverse, many have yet to cultivate an environment that is *truly inclusive*. To reap the full value of diversity there needs to be a concerted effort to ensure inclusion of *everyone*, because diversity does not by itself guarantee inclusion.

Question 13 considers the value of involving team members in strategic aspects that relate to the team (linked to **Tool 1.7 Strategic Thinking**). Giving team members a chance to think about the bigger picture provides them with a better understanding about the 'what' and the 'why' and helps to ensure common ground. It provides an opportunity to keep the team engaged and potentially to gain valuable input, as per Ken Blanchard's wise quote "None of us is as smart as all of us."

Question 15 addresses psychological safety - a concept relatively new to the corporate world but nevertheless hugely important. Team members feel psychologically safe when there is a common understanding that no one will be humiliated or penalised for voicing ideas or opinions, asking questions, giving or seeking feedback, asking for help or admitting errors. To achieve this, conditions need to be created that remove the fear of being disrespected, excluded, ridiculed or fired. If the aim is for employees to bring their best selves to work, then leaders need to create working environments that are psychologically safe. In 2012 Google launched a company-wide study called Project Aristotle to figure out what factors influenced their most successful teams. They found that psychological safety was *by far the most important* in accomplishing team alignment and productivity.[8]

When introducing this tool to coachees I take care to frame questions 11, 13 and 15 in accordance with the descriptions above. With psychological safety being new to many, a few questions such as these help to trigger some advance thinking on the part of the coachee:

- What do you know about how safe team members feel around you?
- Are they comfortable asking when they do not understand or know something in team meetings?
- How do you react when mistakes are made?

---

8 What Google learned from its quest to build the perfect team, 2016, The New York Times Magazine, Charles Duhigg.

"Being a leader has a lot to do with helping other people achieve what they can achieve."

Christine Lagarde

1.10 Situational Leadership

Leadership

Leadership behaviour that is effective in one context may not be effective in another, and this is widely referred to as *Situational Leadership*. The situational leadership Model* below centres on the premise that leaders need to adapt their style to the level of **competence** (ability, knowledge) and **commitment** (confidence, motivation) of their team members, given a certain situation.

*Based on Situational Leadership, Hersey and Blanchard

To note:

- The level of competence and commitment may differ for the same person depending on the task/work to be performed.

- Situations change over time, and so a leader's style will need to adapt accordingly.

- When commitment and competence are high, team members will be demotivated by a directing (micro-managing) style.

- Team members with a high level of commitment but low competence in a certain area will need active coaching and encouragement to succeed.

- When competency is high and commitment is low, the leader needs to demonstrate support, seek to understand what is blocking and involve the team member.

- Regardless of required style, it remains the leader's responsibility to set clear goals and expectations, stay connected to their team members and give continuous feedback.

The best way to be certain about the level of competence and commitment of individual team members is to ask them, rather than relying on one's own assumptions. Asking open questions will reveal both to you as leader *and* to your team members where they stand and what kind of support they need from you in order to succeed.

Assignment:
Think of some different situations with individual team members and use the questions below to guide your thinking. Write your answers in a separate note.

1. **What is the task?**

2. **What do you know about the team member's level of commitment for this task?**

3. **What do you know about the team member's level of competence for this task?**

4. **What open questions could you ask to find out more about their commitment and/or competence?**

5. **What leadership style do you think is most appropriate for the given situation?** (refer to the diagram)

6. **How specifically will you approach this and when?**

7. **How will you follow up?**

Once you have completed the preparation, please try out your identified approach with your team member(s) before our next session.

About Tool 1.10 Situational Leadership

Leadership is contextual (see **Tool 1.4 Six Leadership Styles**). The Situational Based Model developed by Hersey and Blanchard is one of the pioneering leadership theories, stipulating that there is no one superior style of leadership independent of the situation at hand. The model views the performance of followers as a function of *commitment* and *competence,* and places the responsibility to adapt to the situation *on the leader*.

This model is helpful for coachees to think about what potential blocking factors may be preventing their team members from meeting certain performance expectations. It encourages a more mindful diagnosis of issues rather than relying solely on initial assumptions. This can often uncover new ways of approaching issues that in turn leads to more constructive interactions and better outcomes with team members.

How to use the tool

Most senior executives are by now largely familiar with the term *situational leadership*. I use this model to drill down further into this aspect of leadership which has usually been addressed previously with **Tool 1.4 Six Leadership Styles**. Here the focus of the coaching is on 'business as usual' challenges around performance that the coachee faces with team members.

>>

Once the coachee has understood the model, I ask them to complete the exercise using a few real case scenarios and then to try out their conclusions with the individual team members as homework for the following session. In addition to addressing performance issues, this exercise also presents the coachee with the valuable opportunity to practise asking open questions, as they seek to get to the root of team members' non-performance.

It is so important to encourage coachees to turn their intellectual understanding into action and practise tailoring their style to the particular situation and/or team member. As they try out the new approaches, it is beneficial for them to discuss their experiences (positive and negative) with the coach to increase their confidence in adapting their style to the situation at hand.

"Identify your problems but give your power and energy to solutions."

Anthony Robbins

1.11 Solution Orientation

Leadership

How solution-oriented are we when faced with a problem? Once the problem has been identified and its root causes are clearly understood, do we continue to think in terms of *problems* or *solutions*?

Being problem- or solution-orientated are mindsets that we can choose with awareness. The more we orient our mind to solutions, the less stuck we remain in problems. Understanding this is useful for ourselves and also enables us to influence others (our team/s, stakeholders) to adopt a more constructive approach to problem solving.

Below are some questions that shift our thinking from problems to solutions:

- ✓ *What would we like to make happen?*

- ✓ *How will we know when we have achieved it?*

- ✓ *How can we work around the obstacles we have identified?*

- ✓ *What benefits and opportunities will this solution bring?*

- ✓ *What are other perspectives that could be useful when thinking about this?*

- ✓ *Who can help us?*

- ✓ *What are similar circumstances where we have succeeded in the past?*

- ✓ *What is the learning here?*

- ✓ *What will our next immediate step be?*

Reflection Point:

What opportunities do you have to practise a focused, solution-oriented approach to problem solving for yourself and with others?

_____

_____

_____

About Tool 1.11 Solution Orientation

Dealing with problems is a vital part of business. However, leaders need to be alert that constant problem solving and so called 'firefighting' can rapidly become an overriding part of the culture, and thereby get in the way of other important factors such as creating and communicating a compelling vision, nurturing talent, developing strategy and managing stakeholders.

It is easy to get stuck in overthinking and brooding about problems and spend far too much time in a negative frame of mind. Once the problem is diagnosed and understood, the way around this is to consciously turn our attention to *how we would like things to be*. This shift to thinking about a positive outcome focuses the brain on to future possibilities instead of the problem itself. When we are clear about the outcome we want, creative energy is released and it becomes quicker and easier to brainstorm potential solutions and make decisions.

Since problem orientation is the natural go-to mode for most people, it can be challenging to shift one's attention without some reference as support. This tool gives coachees that reference and again demonstrates just how powerful asking the right questions can be.

How to use the tool

I offer this tool to coachees who I feel may benefit from a more solution-oriented approach for themselves, their team and/or with their stakeholders.

To familiarise the coachee with the tool, I ask them to think of a problem where the root cause has been diagnosed and describe that problem to me. I then ask the coachee a selection or all the questions in the tool (depending on the nature of the problem). As I ask the questions the energy in the room will usually start to change as the coachee's motivation around the topic increases - and it is extraordinary to witness how quickly this can happen. When exploring possibilities from a solution- rather than a problem-oriented perspective, we are using parts of our brain that generate an elevated state within us. In this state, thinking outside the box and connecting the dots is easier; and as an added bonus it has an infectious effect on those around us.

I usually ask the coachee to commit to practising this in a setting of their choice and then share their experiences in the next coaching session.

"To lead people, walk beside them. As for the best leaders, the people do not notice their existence.... When the best leader's work is done the people say, 'We did it ourselves'!"

Lao Tzu

1.12 One-to-One Coaching Meetings

Leadership

The focus of these meetings is the individual team member's professional development (as opposed to operational status checkpoint). Therefore, in order to create value each meeting needs to be positioned as *the team member's meeting*. This will be reflected in the way it is conducted, with the manager doing roughly 80% of the listening and only 20% of the talking.

It is beneficial to have a structure that remains consistent for every meeting and where only the content changes, since everyone knows what to expect and how to prepare accordingly. The frequency for this type of one-to-one is usually monthly but may vary depending on the team.

Here is an example of meeting agenda headlines to create your own structure with your direct reports.

1. **Overall status update and review since the last one-to-one (team member)**
   (Big picture: achievements, challenges, reflections)

2. **Observations since the last one-to-one (leader)**
   (Recognition, constructive feedback)

3. **Review of upcoming *priorities* (team member)**
   (The big line priorities between current and next catch-up)

4. **Team member's topic(s)**
   (Team member's issues, concerns, need for clarification)

5. **Your coaching topic(s) for the team member**
   (Agree one area of improvement on which to actively coach your team member. Agree actions to be reviewed in next meeting.)

6. **Yearly objectives review**
   (One per quarter)

7. **Any other business**
   (For example company/departmental information)

Tips:
- Take time to prepare each meeting.
- Seek to ask open questions.
- End each one-to-one on a positive note.
- Let the team member summarise the agreed actions and send them to you shortly after each meeting.
- Keep a folder for each team member of actions and commitments made.

Assignment:
Please send me your agenda structure for one-to-one coaching meetings prior to our next session.

About Tool 1.12 One-to-One Coaching Meetings

One-to-one coaching-style meetings between managers and their direct reports can reap considerable benefits. They give team members focused time with a manager who is personally invested in them and their development; and by the same token they provide managers with the possibility to offer tailored support, foster trust, set clear expectations and provide timely feedback. They also give managers the chance to develop their coaching skills by learning to be fully present, actively listen, ask open questions, challenge and guide their team members.

Executives who consider one-to-one coaching meetings a priority will come well prepared and be committed to keeping these meetings in their calendar. This will significantly contribute to creating an environment where their team members feel valued, engaged and motivated to perform well.

Most people managers do have one-to-ones with their direct reports because it is now a requirement in the majority of companies. However, these meetings are mostly of an operational nature where tasks and issues are addressed and ticked off.

One-to-one coaching-style meetings that focus on the individual team member's development and growth are rarer, and if they do exist they usually lack structure, making the value they generate questionable. It became apparent to me early on that most coachees are eager to improve the way they develop their people, but they frequently struggle to know where to begin. Having a headlined agenda is often the catalyst required to get them thinking about a structure that is relevant to their team and the nature of their business.

How to use the tool

Tool 2.1 Leading the Team and related coaching conversations will reveal a lot about how the coachee interacts with their teams and direct reports.

If the coaching moves to team member development and the coachee wants to implement (or improve) one-to-one coaching-style catch-ups, I ask questions based around what is currently happening, what they would like to happen and how these differ. I will also encourage the coachee to consider what the agenda headlines could be. Finally, if I feel that the coachee may benefit from some more support to fuel their creativity, I ask if they are interested in looking at this tool to help create their own.

"No matter how brilliant your mind or strategy, if you're playing a solo game you'll always lose out to a team."

Reid Hoffman

1.13 Team Meetings

Leadership

Are your team meetings producing the outcomes you want? How do your team members feel about them? Do they value the meetings because they believe time is well spent or do they drag themselves to them?

Team meetings should be something everyone in the team looks forward to: a space where they can contribute and collaborate by sharing ideas and concerns, ask questions, gather important information and have a sense of belonging.

A compelling team meeting agenda is focused on topics that impact the entire team. (Individual discussions should be addressed in one-to-ones or smaller concerned groups.)

Here is an example of a team agenda to inspire you to create your own for regular team meetings. It is useful to create a structure with headlines that can remain the same for each meeting: this way everyone knows what to expect and how to prepare accordingly.

1. **Recent wins and recognitions since last meeting (leader - 5 minutes)**
   (Accomplishments of team and/or individual efforts)

2. **High level status update (leader - 5 minutes)**
   (Brief and concise. Share the 'why' behind decisions, actions and expectations)

3. **Review of team *priorities* and progress (all - 10 minutes)**
   (What is working and what is not; ensuring that the team is on track)

4. **Team topics: ideas, solutions, challenges, troubleshooting (all - 20 minutes)**
   (Team member topics, sharing, brainstorming that involves everyone in the team)

5. **Next Steps (all - 5 minutes)**
   (Summarise agreed actions, owners and target dates)

6. **Any other business (leader - 10 minutes)**
   (Company updates and a few minutes of Q&A from the team)

Tips:
- Take time to prepare each meeting.
- Set a realistic amount of time for each agenda topic.
- Take turns to lead the meeting (time-keeping, keeping the team focused on the agreed topics).
- Make sure that everyone participates.
- Ban personal screens.
- To keep team members *focused on topic*, ask when required: "How is this relevant to the agenda point we are discussing?" or "How does that add value to this conversation?"
- Make decisions while you are together as a team.
- Ensure actions, owners and target dates are distributed after each meeting.

- Make use of a 'parking lot' for ideas that are not part of the meeting agenda. This is a good way to keep the meeting on track without losing unrelated but important points that may come up.
- End each team meeting on a positive note.
- Seek feedback from the team about the quality of the meetings - what works well/not so well - and tweak accordingly.

Assignment:
Send me your agenda structure for the regular team meetings prior to our next session.

About Tool 1.13 Team Meetings

Team meetings are central in a team setting: this is where topics are debated, ideas exchanged, brainstormings conducted and decisions made that move things forward. They are instrumental in cultivating a collective drive and sense of belonging. A team can only be high-performing if it is aligned around a common vision, and well run team meetings are a perfect vehicle to continuously secure that alignment. They give the leader of the team a consistent platform to communicate the vision/direction and why team members' contribution towards it is important.

Unfortunately far too many meetings are run ineffectively, to the point that they become painful to attend. Some of the reasons for their lack of effectiveness are:

- Lack of agenda or meeting objective(s)
- No agreement about actions, owners, follow-up and next steps
- Lack of active participation and interaction by everyone
- Meeting dominated by a few 'usual suspects'
- Lack of focus
- No out-of-the-box thinking
- No decisions made
- Getting off the topic
- Poor managing of difficult behaviour
- Meeting lasts too long

Not surprisingly this contributes to frustration and disengagement among team members and may sometimes even result in attrition of the most talented individuals.

For recurring team meetings (just like recurring one-to-ones), I am a firm believer that agenda headlines should remain the same so that everyone can prepare.

How to use the tool

Improving the quality of recurring team meetings is a common coaching topic. Once the coaching uncovers the meeting pain points and what the coachee would like to improve, the coachee is invited to consider a better structure and suggest meeting agenda headlines.

Similar to **Tool 1.12 One-to-One Coaching Meetings**, if a template example could be useful as a starting point for thinking, I ask if the coachee is interested to receive this tool. In addition to the agenda example I draw attention to the tips listed in the tool because they are instrumental in leading effective and productive meetings and easy to implement.

>>

To note:

Everyone knows how important preparation is for most business activities, and in particular when it comes to activities involving external clients; but this is often largely overlooked when it comes to internal meetings - especially recurring ones. It is not uncommon for people to move from one meeting to the next without even knowing the topic of that meeting! Therefore, if it seems appropriate, I like to remind coachees about the importance of preparation and will often share what has become a favourite mantra that I picked up somewhere years ago, referred to as 'the 5 Ps': Prior Preparation Prevents Poor Performance.

One of the biggest pain points in recurring meetings is the failure to stick to the agenda; and because this is key to leading effective meetings, I especially zoom in on the 6th bullet point in the *Tips* part of the tool and encourage thinking about how to improve this element.

———————

"Individually, we are one drop. Together, we are an ocean."

Ryunosuke Satoro

———————

1.14 Team Meetings Assessment

Leadership

To make sure team meetings are run effectively and producing desired outcomes, it is worthwhile to assess this process regularly, by oneself and also with the team.

The questions below provide guidance in this assessment:

✓ *Is everyone coming prepared and ready to participate?*

✓ *Are people generally focused or distracted?*

✓ *Do team members get equal opportunity to participate and are all opinions and ideas being heard?*

✓ *Are we exchanging on the right agenda topics?*

✓ *Are problems getting solved?*

✓ *Is the team taking concrete decisions?*

✓ *Are we being effective in managing follow-up actions and target dates?*

✓ *Are the meetings stimulating and challenging?*

✓ *What is the level of engagement when we meet?*

✓ *Where is there room for improvement?*

About Tool 1.14 Team Meeting Assessment

It is easy to get complacent with routines and something that has worked well in the past may have lost momentum over time. Therefore, stepping back regularly to assess the effectiveness of recurring meetings is well worthwhile.

This tool supports the coachee to think broadly about the quality of their meetings. For the assessment to be meaningful it should cover behaviours and overall meeting dynamics (interactions and exchanges), as well as the relevance of the agenda points covered.

How to use the tool

I recommend that the coachee first completes the assessment themselves and then engages their team members to do the same exercise. The differences in perception are highly beneficial to sharpen and adjust the meetings in order to keep them relevant and dynamic.

"Probably my best quality as a coach is that I ask a lot of questions and let the person come up with the answers."

Phil Dixon

1.15 Coaching-Style Questions

Leadership

Remember to be present and listen with engagement:

- ✓ *What has gone well since our last one-to-one/team meeting?*

- ✓ *What have you learned?*

- ✓ *Is there anything you would have done differently?*

- ✓ *What is the best possible outcome that you are aiming for?*

- ✓ *How have you determined your priorities?*

- ✓ *How does this support the team vision?*

- ✓ *What is the key thing you want to improve moving forward?*

- ✓ *Are there any blocking factors standing in the way of you doing your job well?*

- ✓ *What kind of support do you need from me?*

- ✓ *Do you have suggestions for improving the way we work together?*

- ✓ *What do you need to do to ensure you have the outcomes you are expecting?*

- ✓ *How will you know when you have succeeded?*

- ✓ *How will you maintain momentum?*

- ✓ *What will your next step be?*

- ✓ *Overall in our team what do you think is most important, and how do you think we are doing?*

- ✓ *What am I not noticing, and if you were in my position what would you do about it?*

Listen to their answers without interrupting. Then respond honestly, being generous with your appreciation, and remain as focused and specific as you can with any constructive negative feedback. In an environment where people feel valued and heard and clearly understand what is required from them and why, they will be motivated to make changes.

About Tool 1.15 Coaching-Style Questions

Coaching-style questions are a trigger for deeper thinking to help people find their own answers and solutions. The aim of this tool is to support executives to raise awareness and instil a sense of ownership in their teams. Questions that are open-ended and asked with curiosity help to foster ownership, autonomy and engagement in team members. However, for most people it is not so straightforward to ask open questions: it does not come naturally.

I devised this list of questions - which is by no means exhaustive - as a guide to encourage coachees to increasingly use open-ended questions when they are coaching, guiding, supporting and mentoring their teams.

How to use the tool

For coachees keen to develop their coaching skills, learning to lead by questions is central. Since doing this may feel unnatural at first, I encourage the coachee to spend some time thinking about what they want to accomplish and considering the open questions they could ask to find this out. I offer the coachee the set of questions in this tool as a starting point for them to become more familiar with open-ended questioning. The aim is for them to start formulating and practise using their own coaching-style questions so that this becomes increasingly part of their leadership approach.

"An organization's ability to learn, and translate that learning into action rapidly, is the ultimate competitive advantage."

Jack Welch

1.16 Developing the Team

Leadership

Please reflect on the development of your team members by letting the questions below guide your thinking:

1. **What do you know about your team members' individual interests and aspirations when it comes to learning and development?**

    _____
    _____
    _____

2. **How would you describe the current skillset level in the team? Is it where you need the team to be in order to achieve your vision?**

    _____
    _____
    _____

3. **What skills will be required in the immediate, mid- and long-term that the team currently does not have?** (Please explain the gap)

    _____
    _____
    _____

4. **What is your plan and approach to develop these skills with your low, medium and high performers?**

    _____
    _____
    _____

5. **What additional opportunities to develop the team members could be available to you?** (Courses, new tasks, delegation, mentoring, collaboration on projects, cross-functional, industry forums, etc.)

    _____
    _____
    _____

6. **Where are you with regards to succession planning?**

    _____
    _____
    _____

About Tool 1.16 Developing the Team

In today's fast-moving world, opportunities for learning are in high demand among employees: professional development has become a key strategy for building an attractive and lasting career. Having a highly skilled and capable workforce is of course also essential to the continued success and sustainability of any organisation, making a solid employee development framework a win-win for both parties. Over time, people managers have become increasingly responsible for professional development, talent retention and succession planning in their respective areas; and these managers have a big impact on how employees view their development opportunities. People managers who understand their team members' strengths, value their input and encourage their growth are much more likely to retain talent.

Yet even though it is generally accepted that training and development are essential to develop high performing teams, most managers are not sufficiently consistent in spending time to really understand the specific needs, capabilities, interests and motivations of their team members. They frequently need reminding that their success as leaders very much depends on the capabilities and performance of their team. In reality, 'business as usual' (BAU) demands frequently get in the way of people development.

How to use the tool

When team development is on the coaching agenda, this tool is useful for the coachee to think about:

- Whether the team members are on track in relation to their objectives.

- Whether the coachee knows the team members' ambitions and development needs.

- Whether the current plan needs adjustment.

It also puts the spotlight on succession planning, which is far too often overlooked. Reasons for not having a proper succession plan vary from being distracted by BAU to being fearful of team members posing a threat to the coachee's own position should they develop the team's potential. The coaching conversation is effective in identifying, exploring and resolving any such issues.

"Make feedback normal.
Not a performance review."

Ed Batista

1.17 Delivering Feedback

Leadership

Most of us are reluctant to deliver feedback and will therefore often shy away from giving it, choosing comfort over courage. However, the consequence of non-action will often result in issues not being resolved as well as potential increase of tension and resentment.

Having a structure for delivering feedback is therefore most helpful. *The Three-Part Message*[9] provides a simple and highly effective framework for giving both negative and positive feedback.

The Three-Part Message Components

1. **Separate the Person from the Problem**
   Describe the problem or behaviour in a *brief*, factual and non-judgemental manner. Do not get personal or share your own interpretations; stick to describing what you have observed.

   +

2. **Communicate Your Feelings**
   Describe how that problem/behaviour makes you feel.

   +

3. **Describe the Wider Effect**
   Describe the tangible consequence the problem/behaviour has on you and/or your team.

The Three-Part Message Conversation

"When you [describe the problem/behaviour non-judgmentally], **I feel** [communicate your feelings] **because** [describe the effect on you]."

Examples:

1. When you are frequently late to our meetings + the rest of us feel disrespected + because our valuable time is wasted while waiting for you.

2. When you don't verify your work before giving it to me + I feel frustrated + because I end up staying later in the office correcting your mistakes and miss out on valuable evening time with my family.

To Note:

✓ The Three-Part Message demonstrates how the final piece (describing the wider effect) is essential because people are often not aware about the consequences of their behaviour or actions on others. When they become aware they are much more willing to take ownership and corrective action.

✓ The Three-Part Message structure is *also effective when giving positive feedback.*

Assignment:
Think of two to three upcoming situations where it would be useful to apply this structure. Write your Three-Part Messages in a separate note and send to me prior to our next session. Keep it simple.

---

9 Developed by Thomas Gordon

About Tool 1.17 Delivering Feedback

Delivering feedback in a constructive way without feeling overwhelmed by stress, fear and guilt is an important aspect of leadership and one of the most popular coaching topics - because it is one of the hardest things executives need to do. The reasons for unease range from cultural background to wanting to be liked, to the fear of hurting others, to not wanting to demotivate team members. Nevertheless, giving feedback regularly and as close to the occurrence as possible is important because what people are unaware of they simply cannot change or improve. This may sound obvious but it is something that is often forgotten, mostly because the person who should give the feedback is submerged in their own feelings about the situation.

The Three-Part Message was originally formulated to support people to develop skills around assertiveness. I immediately fell in love with its simplicity and effectiveness and decided to test it as a structure for giving feedback as well. It is a wonderful tool that gives the coachee the courage to give feedback to their team members and to easily integrate this skill into their leadership. Even though the primary focus in coaching is around giving negative feedback, the Three-Part Message is also effective for giving positive feedback as it gives the recipient more detail about their positive performance, in addition to "Good work, thank you."

The structure is very effective on its own for 'lighter' occurrences such as the examples given in the tool. When it comes to more in-depth conversations aimed at developing and growing people, then a longer conversation as outlined in **Tool 1.18 Preparing a Feedback Conversation** is preferable.

How to use the tool

At the outset I like to remind coachees that if people are not aware of an issue due to lack of feedback, they cannot change or improve.

Then I usually ask the coachee to take me through what is currently happening for them around this topic. Blocking factors that show why the coachee finds this hard will surface fairly quickly, and the coaching will seek to clear (or at least minimise) these factors.

To deliver feedback well, I point out how preparation goes a long way (see *The 5 Ps* in the text box of **Tool 1.13 Team Meetings**). Having gone through the Three-Part Message in the safe space the coaching provides, most coachees are eager to start working with it. To get comfortable with the flow of the message structure, I ask them to prepare and send me a few different completed scenarios as homework. Then in the following session they will practise their messages with me in order to fine-tune them and also to be mindful about congruence in their nonverbal communication.

"The growth and development of people is the highest calling of leadership."

Harvey S. Firestone

1.18 Preparing a Feedback Conversation

Leadership

A key aspect of being a leader is supporting people's development and growth, and feedback is one of the most effective ways for individuals to improve their performance and develop their skills.

There are several ways to conduct a feedback conversation. Here is a structure focused on mindful preparation and incorporating the Three-Part Message:

1. Calm your emotions
While it is important that feedback is delivered as close to the occurrence as possible, it is not constructive to do so when feeling angry or upset. If your emotions are running high it is best to let things cool down so you can think about the situation more clearly.

2. Consider your motive
Make sure your intention is appropriate - that is to be helpful, supportive and to *develop* the individual. If this is not the case, then you may wish to reconsider giving the feedback.

3. Prepare a balanced message
Start with the person's specific strengths that are relevant to the conversation. This acknowledges them and their value and reinforces the things the person should keep doing.

Write down your concern in line with the Three-Part Message structure so that you are clear about the issue and the reason for giving the feedback. Make sure the message is thoughtful and free from accusations and assumptions and that it is actionable (the person can do something about it). Give a few specific recent examples to illustrate the first part of the Three-Part Message where factual observation is shared.

Determine *how* you are going to deliver the message and rehearse it several times to increase your confidence and effectiveness.

Anticipate likely reactions and responses and prepare for them as well.

4. Deliver the feedback
Never deliver negative feedback in front of others: find a private place to conduct these types of conversations. Remain calm and avoid small talk as it can easily dilute the seriousness of the message. Take care that your nonverbal communication (posture, eye contact, pace of speech, tone, facial expressions, gestures) is congruent with your message. Keep your voice calm and firm.

Examples of opening sentences can be:
"I have some thoughts/feedback I would like to share with you - would you like to hear it?"
"Can I share some observations with you?"

5. Be silent and listen

After delivering your message be silent and allow the other person to process what you have said. Do not interrupt or argue, just listen with the intention to understand.

6. Repeat steps 4 - 5 as many times as necessary

Expect that the other person may get defensive and that this is understandable. Then restate the identical Three-Part Message again. Do not allow yourself to get side-tracked: the other person may try to get off topic by changing the subject. Let them know that other points can be discussed at a later time and that right now the focus is on this one issue. Steps 4 and 5 may need to be repeated several times before the other person has really heard and understood what you want to convey.

Calm persistence goes a long way.

7. Focus on the solution

Have a dialogue and, where possible, let the person propose a solution; and if a solution is proposed, make sure it meets your needs. Paraphrase to ensure mutual understanding.

8. Support and follow-up

Ask how you can best support the person moving forward. If appropriate, agree on a time for follow-up. This establishes accountability and increases the probability of improvement.

9. End on a positive note

Conclude with a positive and encouraging comment and thank the person.

Assignment:

Please prepare and conduct at least one conversation prior to our next session.

About Tool 1.18 Preparing a Feedback Conversation

Naturally there are several approaches to conducting feedback conversations. This structure helps the coachee prepare and think through their motive for giving the feedback, consider how to deliver it and also anticipate responses and reactions from the recipient. The preparation increases the coachee's chances of remaining calm, constructive and confident throughout the conversation.

The specific person and situation will determine whether a full conversation is required. There are times when it will be sufficient to deliver the Three-Part Message on its own (as per the examples given in **Tool 1.17 Delivering Feedback**). Longer feedback conversations are typically better when the objective is to develop the individual.

How to use the tool

I ask the coachee to select a topic that makes sense to use in a full conversation. The coaching will then centre on the coachee reflecting on each step in the tool. Again having a structure to refer to and be able to think out loud will usually significantly reduce stress and anxiety, and enable the coachee to tap into a more resourceful state.

>>

To note:

Point 3. A balanced message that incorporates strengths, the issue of concern and ending on an encouraging note is sometimes referred to as the 'sandwich approach'. I am a strong supporter of this approach when it comes to helping people develop their skills, potential and performance: the motive is not to break the person's confidence so that they end up doubting themselves and their capabilities, but rather to support them to address areas of improvement and blind spots. A balanced message helps to reinforce confidence and keep weak areas in perspective.

As the coachee anticipates reactions and responses from the recipient of the feedback, I may (re-) introduce **Tool 2.1 The Communication Process** to help focus on likely outcomes.

Point 4. Since it can be challenging to get into the feedback part, I have added two examples of opening sentences. They ask for permission to share, thereby extending respect and helping the individual to be receptive to the feedback; it is an effective way to enter into the critique. Once we have the start, the rest follows more easily.

Point 6. Receiving negative feedback can be very tough: it is a blow to our ego and sense of identity, and hence the immediate reaction is to want to defend ourselves. Our brains are biologically wired to protect ourselves when we perceive an attack and our natural instinct is 'fight or flight', so it is important to remember that defensiveness is natural and therefore OK, and to take it into account during the preparation in order to remain calm throughout the conversation.

The coachee will be asked to prepare and deliver at least one conversation prior to the following coaching session where the focus will be on reviewing their experience and take-aways. Again for most coaches to become skilful and comfortable in conducting these conversations, practice and recalibration when required is necessary.

"Teamwork is working together, even when apart."

Anonymous

"Teamwork begins by building trust. And the only way to do that is to overcome our need for invulnerability."

Patrick Lencioni

1.19 Leading Remotely

Leadership

Please reflect and answer the questions below:

1. **What do you consider to be most challenging when leading remotely?**

   _____

   _____

2. **What do you know about your team members' experiences of being led by you when working remotely?** (How connected, included, informed and supported do they feel?)

   _____

   _____

3. **How would you describe the level of collaboration and mutual support when team members work remotely?**

   _____

   _____

4. **What specifically are you doing to safeguard the team spirit and culture?**

   _____

   _____

5. **How are you managing the risk of loneliness/depression/burn-out in the team?** (mental health)

   _____

   _____

6. **How are work priorities managed, how is progress monitored, and how are team members held accountable?**

   _____

   _____

7. **How do you ensure information (company and team) is shared regularly and in a timely manner?**

   _____

   _____

8. **What would you optimise in the current structure to better meet your own and the team's needs and expectations?**

   _____

   _____

About Tool 1.19 Leading Remotely

When the COVID-19 lockdown happened, my clients fell into two groups: those who already had experience of leading teams located in other locations and those who were leading remotely for the first time. The first group had an advantage, yet had never experienced a situation where everyone - including themselves - was confined to their homes for an indefinite period.

The lockdown triggered a whole range of questions: How do we keep everyone safe? How can we continue to operate our business as seamlessly as possible? How do I manage myself so that I can be resourceful for those I lead? How do I connect regularly without being seen as micro-managing? How do I demonstrate empathy? How do we make goals outcome-based? What do I need to change about the way I delegate? How do I hold team members accountable? How do I nurture our team spirit and sense of belonging? What do I need to do to become more trusting? So many things to consider...

One of the biggest issues for executives when it comes to staff working away from the office is around trust: trust that people really work when they are not being physically supervised. Research into remote working (pre-COVID-19) dispelled the assumption that people would lie around watching Netflix all day instead of working. Quite the contrary: it shows that companies who offer flexible, well-structured solutions can reap significant benefits such as improved employee wellbeing, reduced absenteeism and increased engagement, productivity and talent retention.

While a few people may abuse it, the vast majority respond really well to trust; so it hardly seems logical or fair to prohibit remote working because of a minority of abusers. The COVID-19 confinement - the largest remote working occurrence of our time - left most companies completely unprepared and with no choice but to extend trust to their employees. This experience confirms the research: employees can work productively from home and can be trusted to do so. This is why most organisations now accept that remote working will be integral to the evolution of the workplace: hybrid models will be the future. For companies who do not have a history and culture of remote working prior to COVID-19, new frameworks will need to be created drawing on lessons and insights from the confinement. These frameworks will need to be carefully designed to incorporate trust, outcome-based goals, regular communication, empowerment, active support, full inclusion, accountability, attention to life balance (switching off outside working hours) and last, but not least, attention to mental health.

This tool was created in the lockdown period to support clients to figure out how best to lead their teams remotely and also in preparation for a new paradigm around the 'future of work'.

How to use the tool

Leading remotely undoubtedly adds an additional layer of complexity to the challenges of leadership. The questions in this tool encourage the coachee to think about relevant key aspects from a wide perspective.

To note:

Question 4 addresses the importance of safeguarding team spirit and a sense of belonging. Here a genuine engagement and some creativity are required. Internal company surveys show that after a day of work and virtual meetings, employees are only motivated to get on another call if it is informal, light and an opportunity for fun and laughter. I hear about a number of virtual initiatives my clients have implemented, from pizza lunches and quizzes to after-work drinks and dress-up themes. Managing this is not as easy as it may sound and requires real effort from leaders/managers to get it right. It is important to ensure that everyone is included and has a chance to participate so that the get-togethers are not dominated by the usual few. However, what works for one team may not work for all, so it is about trying things out and evaluating the results together with the team.

>>

In some of my client get-togethers business talk is completely off the table; and this has led to team members getting to know each other better than in pre-COVID times! Another client of mine has implemented weekly spontaneous drop-ins, where he opens his virtual room for a while and team members can 'drop in' for an informal, agenda-free chat. Having this forum has produced an added benefit for him: it draws his attention to those people who seldom or never show up, and this prompts him to check in on them individually to find out how they are doing (see note on Question 5 below).

In addition to virtual get-togethers, taking care to celebrate wins and give praise when projects and goals are completed goes a long way to nurturing team spirit and that all-important sense of belonging.

Question 5 draws attention to the mental health aspect of longer-term remote working. Human beings are social creatures: connecting with others and feeling cared-for are essential to our well-being. Therefore, checking in on individual team members with compassion and empathy to understand how they are coping is a significant aspect of leading remotely. To get beyond the answer "I'm OK", it is often helpful if the leader can demonstrate their own vulnerability by sharing something they themselves are struggling with. This sends a strong message of "It's OK not to feel OK" and will encourage team members to reveal how they really feel. For the conversation to be meaningful it is important that the leader listens deeply to understand how best to offer support.

One of my clients in charge of a high pressure operational environment has implemented periodic sessions where the team can vent their frustrations together. This is a good way to get everything out, brainstorm solutions once the problems have been identified (**Tool 1.11 Solution Orientation** can be used here) and end on a supportive, constructive note.

One positive aspect of COVID-19 that I have observed is that the stigma around mental health has rapidly reduced. I am finding leaders increasingly open to engage on this collective human aspect and mindful about finding solutions to help employees stay mentally and emotionally healthy in turbulent times.

"It's important to make sure that we're talking with each other in a way that heals, not in a way that wounds."

Barack Obama

1.20 Communicating in Uncertainty

Leadership

In times of change, uncertainty and crisis, people will instinctively look to their leaders for direction and stability. Communicating on a regular basis, even when it feels like there is nothing much to say, is crucial to preserve employees' trust, loyalty and motivation; and it also helps to minimise unnecessary rumours and speculation.

Demonstration of caring and authentically crafted communication builds trust and a sense of belonging that is critical to securing people's buy-in and support. It accentuates a shared underlying mission that says "We are all in this together."

Example of a useful structure:

1. **"This is what we know as of today ...."**
   (Focus on the facts and be truthful: this builds trust.)

2. **"Here is what we currently don't know ...."**
   (Be as transparent as you can and share the uncertainties.)

3. **"I think that....... and I feel ...."**
   (Convey your empathy, let them know how you feel and (if appropriate) demonstrate your own vulnerability around what is happening.)

4. **"My commitment is ...."**
   (Let them know what you commit to do.)

5. **"Here is what I would like you to do ...."**
   (Communicate your expectations clearly. Ask for their support to come together during this time.)

6. **"Do you have any questions?"**
   (Take care to really listen with the intention to understand and to create openings for dialogue.)

7. **"Thank you for your patience and trust during this time."**
   (End by expressing your gratitude.)

About Tool 1.20 Communicating in Uncertainty

Uncertainty and crisis will naturally trigger fear, stress and anxiety and situations like these often provide the ultimate test of leadership. They require that leaders be increasingly present, demonstrate their humanity, find their compassionate leadership voice and their courage to share their own vulnerabilities around the situation, while at the same time project strength, unity, composure, confidence and hope. There is a lot to take into account.

I first used this tool during the financial crisis in 2008/9 to support my CEO clients at the time. Since then it has been updated and also extended to coachees managing any type of impactful and potentially uncomfortable change. It naturally became relevant again at the outset of COVID-19 - the biggest crisis of our lifetime.

How to use the tool

When coaching on this topic I ask the coachee to put themselves in the shoes of the people they will be addressing and seek to understand and feel what things are like from that perspective. By understanding this perspective it is easier for them to bring forth empathy.

Questions I may ask the coachee to solicit their insights are:

- What do you know about your people's current concerns?
- What issues are they grappling with?
- What are their biggest fears?
- What are they expecting from you now as their leader?

If the coachee has problems answering these questions, it reveals they probably need to connect more with employees and really listen with the intention to understand.

Careful preparation, leading with the facts and demonstrating humanity are all required to deliver an effective message. In these times of considerable social media usage, depending on the situation that is being addressed, it may be worth reminding people to refrain from believing in everything they see on these outlets and to seek out the facts.

Ultimately this kind of communication is about conveying the underlying message that "We are all in this together and we will get through this together." It is an opportunity to establish a stronger, more aligned, better engaged and more loyal workforce.

Effective Communication

"Communication works for those who work at it."

John Powell

About Effective Communication

Communication is the basis of all human interaction. It is how we exchange thoughts, feelings, ideas and information with the words we speak or write, the tone we adopt, the way we listen, the energy we bring, the sounds we make and the gestures we use. Communication is both conscious and unconscious, an emotional transaction that influences reactions and perceptions in the people we interact with. Since absence, silence and withdrawal may give rise to considerable reactions, we are always communicating - whether we are aware of it or not.

You know that you have been part of an effective communication when both parties feel understood; that they experienced a mutually meaningful exchange. This kind of conversation requires mindfulness and a discernment that is frequently lacking, which is why there are so many unnecessary misunderstandings.

To increase your chances of being effective, you first need to become clear about what you want to achieve: your desired outcome as a result of the upcoming interaction. When you have this clarity you then need to consider what the other person's priorities and intentions may be, also taking into account such aspects as their personality, communication style, gender, culture and generation. Preparing with these points in mind will help determine how best to approach the person, situation and topic in order to maximise your impact and influence.

Our mindset, the energy we bring, our ability to listen, to be present, to choose the right words, to be congruent in our nonverbal cues: all these play a central part in determining an interaction's outcome. The way we communicate is an expression of our attitude and greatly influences how we are perceived by the people around us. Understanding that there is no single communication style that will work for every person and situation helps us to consciously refine our own approach and increase our chances of being effective.

Given the central role that communication plays, it is probably the most important skill we have at our disposal in the workplace. It is how we learn, inform, decide and share information between employees, senior management, customers and external stakeholders. Effective communication is the means to setting clear expectations, creating alignment and buy-in around an organisation's values and its goals. It is essential for bridging differences, building trusting relationships at all levels, fostering inclusive, high-performing cultures and achieving desired outcomes.

bryanridgley.com

"Communication is only effective when we communicate in a way that is meaningful to the recipient, not ourselves."

Rich Simmons

2.1 The Communication Process

Communication

The Communication Process

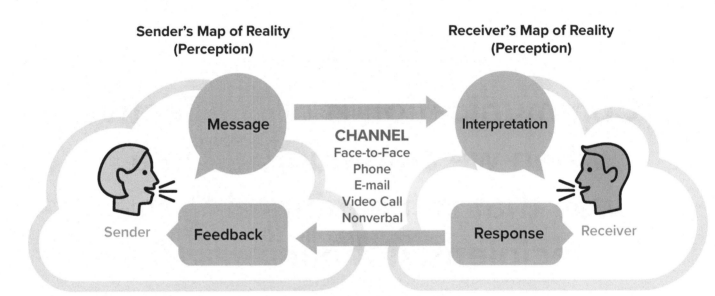

Sender's Map of Reality (Perception)

Receiver's Map of Reality (Perception)

Message

CHANNEL
Face-to-Face
Phone
E-mail
Video Call
Nonverbal

Interpretation

Sender

Feedback

Response

Receiver

CONSIDER:

- What message do I want to convey? (specifically)
- What do I know about the other person, how s/he will best understand or be interested?

- What would I like the other person to feel?
- What actions do I want the other person to take as a result of our interaction?

About Tool 2.1 The Communication Process

The Communication Process is a great place to start coaching for effective communication, as it puts a framework around this very comprehensive topic. The first communication process model was developed in 1948 by Claude Shannon for Bell Laboratories and has since been expanded and developed by numerous people. I have slightly revamped the diagram to emphasise an individual's uniqueness by drawing a separate cloud around the 'Sender' and 'Receiver'.

No two people are the same - not even identical twins. Everyone is unique with their own distinct cloud. Our 'Map of Reality' cloud makes up *who we are* and is composed of everything we have experienced since we were born until the present moment: our upbringing, education, social status, culture, personality traits, nationality, religion, life experiences.... It influences the way we see the world, including how we interpret the things that are said to us and the things that happen to us. In other words, our Map of Reality is synonymous with our perception - the way we perceive the world around us.

If we want to be effective and impactful in our communication we need to consider the other person's cloud - *their reality* - as opposed to coming at things solely from our own perspective and assumptions. However, most of us don't consider this aspect. We usually take for granted that others will understand us and consequently do not give much thought about the recipient or how we communicate, which in turn can easily lead to misunderstanding.

How to use the tool

To frame effective communication, I begin by taking the coachee through the Communication Process, which in theory is a straightforward procedure: the Sender formulates a message, chooses an appropriate channel and sends the message to the Receiver. The Receiver interprets it, chooses an appropriate channel and sends a response back to the Sender. So far, so good.

But as we all know from direct experience, so much can go wrong at any stage of this process:

- The Sender's message may be unclear, ambiguous and/or formulated in a way that is challenging for the Recipient to understand.
- The selected channel may not be appropriate for that particular message.
- The Receiver might be in a bad mood, which may influence the way s/he interprets it.

And so on...

If we have difficulty being understood or understanding somebody else, it is likely some part of the Communication Process has been overlooked. The questions at the bottom of the illustration encourage reflection and help the coachee think about things like:

- Providing the right context (framing the message)
- Ensuring relevance and clarity
- The desired outcome and call to action

How we formulate our communication is equally important to *what* we want to say; this is what is meant by the well-known phrase 'know your audience'. Being mindful of the other person's cloud is key to being relevant, communicating effectively and creating the desired impact and outcome.

The Communication Process is a simple yet profound tool for diagnosing different situations that have occurred as well as preparing for future scenarios. Coachees are quick to embrace it and are soon referring to the clouds in the context of their communication challenges.

I find the model so useful that I will often also introduce it when coaching for other topics that involve interactions with others, such as Leadership, Emotional Intelligence or Stakeholder Management.

"We don't see things as *they* are,
we see them as *we* are."

Anais Nin

2.2 Perception

Communication

Roger N Shepard

What do you see?

Our brains are wired from birth by individual experiences, resulting in every person having their own unique perception of reality. It comes as no surprise then to understand that communication is greatly influenced by perception.

Since our natural tendency is to be emotionally linked to our own perspective (our cloud), we are often unable to consider things more broadly. Being conscious also to take other perspectives into account can help us dissociate emotionally and be more open. Learning to do this is useful when we want to communicate effectively, influence, negotiate, resolve conflict and make better decisions.

Please reflect on these questions and write your answers in a separate note.

1. **How would you rate your current level of awareness and openness to potential differences in perception when you communicate with others?** (on a scale of 1 to 5 with 5 being the highest)

_____

_____

2. **Explain the reason behind the rating you have given yourself.**

_____

_____

3. **As you think about perception in the context of the professional interactions you have, what comes to your mind?**

_____

_____

About Tool 2.2 Perception

As we have established, none of us sees the world from exactly the same viewpoint. Yet interestingly one of the biggest mistakes we make is to assume that other people think the same way we think! In fact there is rarely one absolute truth. There is *your* perception - your truth, based on your life experiences; and then there are the perceptions of everyone else, based on their life experiences. In reality, we all have a piece of the truth.

This tool builds on **Tool 2.1 The Communication Process** and aims to deepen awareness of how communication is heavily influenced by perception, as well as the potential value of our different perspectives that may be missed if we are not open to them.

How to use the tool

I show the coachee the illustration above and ask them what they see. Their answer will be quick: either a woman or a saxophone player; and I will then say that I see the other image. When they see the dual images in the same picture, we can conclude that we are *both* right despite our initial perceptions of the same picture being very different. However, if we did not know that the picture comprises two images, we would likely stand firm on our initial perceptions and try to convince the other of our 'truth'.

The point of this simple exercise is to demonstrate our natural tendency to project our own (partial) perspective and experience as the whole truth, and that we often make assumptions based on just one piece of the whole. Understanding that our perspective has limits, we can strive to be open to the possibility that additional perspectives usually give a more complete picture. Having this mindset greatly facilitates more effective communication with others.

Within this framing the coachee is encouraged to reflect about how this relates to their direct experiences and then to complete the questions prior to the following session.

"To effectively communicate, we must realise that we are all different in the way we perceive the world and use this understanding as a guide to our communication with others."

Anthony Robbins

2.3 Reflecting about Communication

Communication

Think of a recent situation (in a professional context) where you had a *mutually* effective and fruitful communication with another person.

With this interaction in mind, please answer the questions below:

1. What did you and the other person do to ensure a good interaction?

_____

_____

2. How do you know the other person also felt that way?

_____

_____

3. What did the two of you express with your eyes?

_____

_____

4. How would you describe your own and the other person's body language?

_____

_____

5. How did you know that the other person was really listening to you?

_____

_____

6. What kind of questions did you ask each other?

_____

_____

7. What else did you do to make one another feel at ease?

_____

_____

8. Is there anything else you would add to help explain why you rated this communication as mutually effective and fruitful?

_____

_____

About Tool 2.3 Reflecting about Communication

It is easy to take communication for granted: it is something we do a large part of the time we are awake. However, if we stop and think about the things involved when we communicate, we realise that even the simplest social interaction between two people includes an extensive range of elements: speaking, listening and interpreting what is being said, reading body language, interpreting gestures and facial expressions, responding to what has been said, formulating one's thoughts into an appropriate message that the other party will understand, assessing whether one's message has been understood, taking turns talking and listening, determining the level of rapport... There is an enormous amount to consider! By becoming increasingly aware about what is involved, we can become more effective.

Starting with the basics, the objective of this tool is to provide a reference point for the coachee using an actual communication experience. Breaking down the elements of their experience helps to understand why it was successful and provides the coachee with a reference they can return to in order to consciously recreate this in future.

How to use the tool

As I provide context in line with About the Tool above, I usually also refer to **Tool 2.1 The Communication Process** as a reminder. I then ask the coachee to think of a few recent examples when they had a mutually effective and fruitful communication and to name these without going into any details. I then proceed to take the coachee through the tool and ask them to complete the exercise for the following session.

In answering the questions, the coachee will gain clarity around the areas that need particular focus and would be useful to work on in the coaching.

"The most important thing in communication is hearing what isn't said."

Peter F. Drucker

2.4 Nonverbal Communication

Communication

Nonverbal communication is powerful: it can make people feel at ease, encourage open dialogue, build trust, boost collaboration... And it can also do the opposite.

Being alert and sensitive to nonverbal communication can help us understand the impact we have on others, as well as the people we interact with. Nonverbal cues can inform us about the mood of the other person(s), if it is time to change the pace or subject of a conversation, whether the other person is engaged or has switched off, when you have talked long enough and when someone else wants to speak.

Here is a list of the most common nonverbal cues:

Facial Expression
Are you aware of your facial expressions when interacting with others?

Eye Contact
This is a crucial part of communication. However, neither too much eye contact (staring) nor too little (avoidance) is good. Some communication experts recommend intervals of eye contact lasting four to five seconds.

Body Language and Posture
Is your body language aligned with the message you want to convey, the impact you want to make and how you want to be perceived?

Gestures
Gestures help reinforce the message and have the potential to enhance communication.

Voice
Notice how your tone, volume and pace affect how others respond to you. Consider whether you would benefit from adapting them in certain circumstances.

Space
We all have need for physical space. Are you mindful of other people's preferences?

Level of Engagement
Is your level of engagement clearly visible in your nonverbal communication?
What about the people you interact with and their level of engagement?

We can all work on our nonverbal communication. By paying attention to and practising nonverbal cues, you can dramatically improve the effectiveness of your overall communication.

About Tool 2.4 Nonverbal Communication

A substantial portion of our communication is nonverbal and ranges from facial expressions to gestures and the use of space. When we interact with others we are constantly sending and receiving nonverbal cues: every gesture, tone of voice, posture, how much or little eye contact we make conveys something. Differences in cultural backgrounds provide additional complexity, since nonverbal cues may have different meanings depending on a person's origins.

Since the nonverbal part of communication is so important and yet frequently overlooked, the purpose of this tool is to bring it to the forefront of the coachee's mind. It is important to emphasise that paying attention to the nonverbal part is instrumental in effective communication.

How to use the tool

I use this tool as a reference in the coaching session and aide-mémoire for the coachee as they work on aspects of their nonverbal communication. I usually take the coachee briefly through the tool and then coach around the nonverbal cues the coachee identifies need practice. If the coachee wishes, they can practise these cues with me in a safe environment in the first instance and then as homework with colleagues between sessions.

To note:

It is important to highlight the significance of *congruence* between verbal and nonverbal communication. If congruence is lacking and we are sending mixed signals between our words and our body language, there is a big risk that we will be seen as dishonest. When your nonverbal cues match your verbal message, rapport, credibility and trust increase. When they do not it can lead to tension, confusion and mistrust, and this is worth knowing.

Once we become accustomed to observing nonverbal communication, our ability to read it and consciously utilise it for impact grows with practice.

"Seek first to understand, then to be understood."

Stephen Covey

2.5 Levels of Listening

Communication

There are several levels of listening. These are (from highest to lowest):

Open-Minded and Engaged Listening
You listen with the intention to really understand the situation of the speaker. When you listen at this level you are fully present. You leave your own judgements behind and seek to step into the reality-cloud of the other person to view things from their perspective. You resist the urge to offer solutions, defend or explain yourself.

Comparative Listening
You listen to the speaker's words and compare them with your own experiences. You remain in your own reality-cloud and are not fully open to the other person's point of view.

Assumptive Listening
At this level we rely on our own assumptions about how the other person feels and what they will say next. This often results in our interrupting and/or attempting to finish their sentences.

Selective Listening
You listen only to what interests you.

Pretend to listen
You give the appearance of listening but actually do not.

Ignore
You make no effort to listen and you show it.

The appropriate level of listening will depend on the person/situation/topic. An increased awareness about the options available enables us to *consciously choose* the correct level. Attempting to listen at the highest level all of the time is exhausting. However, if the person, situation and/or topic are important and need to be dealt with effectively (business or personal), then it is usually wise to choose the open-minded and engaged level.

Please reflect and complete:

1. What level of listening do you use the majority of the time when interacting with your colleagues?

---

2. What do you think this level of listening says about you? (perception)

---

3. In what circumstances would it be beneficial for you to be more aware about your level(s) of listening?

4. When do you think open-minded and engaged listening is most challenging?

5. What will you do to become a better listener?

About Tool 2.5 Levels of Listening

As noted in **Tool 2.1 The Communication Process**, if we want to be effective communicators then we need to consider the reality-cloud of the other person.

To truly understand another person's reality, we need to be present and open to listening. It is sometimes said that the best communicators are superb listeners; however, I think most would agree that few people are superb listeners. Organisations are full of conversations with low levels of listening, meaning opportunities to connect and learn from one another are not fully capitalised on, important decisions take too long to be made and potential for synergy and innovation often remains unexplored and untapped.

The quality of our listening conveys very precise messages to the people communicating with us, whether we are aware of it or not: our listening skills influence how we are perceived by the people around us. This is useful to know if our aim is to inspire, build strong professional relationships or positively influence key stakeholders.

How to use the tool

Because listening is probably the *most* important communication skill, I will often make the point that with awareness and practice we can become better listeners - starting immediately. Becoming a better listener is all about awareness and commitment. I will present the levels of listening and coach around how they relate to the coachee.

To note:

A common misconception when it comes to open-minded and engaged listening is that in applying it you give up your own position. It is important to clarify that this is not the case: we do not necessarily need to agree with the other person or change our stance. We listen at the highest level to gain useful insights about the other person, as opposed to relying solely on our assumptions (which may be incorrect). When we understand the person and their situation it naturally facilitates more constructive conversation, along with the ability to better influence and achieve the best possible outcomes. When we listen fully with the intention to understand, we are open to find synergies and win-win opportunities.

It is worth noting that when we want to connect with what another person is feeling (see **Tool 3.4 Empathy**), it is the highest level of listening that we need to tap into.

The questions in the tool will usually be given as homework between sessions.

"It's encouraging to know that while we only have one chance at first impressions, rapport can be built all the time."

Unknown

2.6 Rapport

Communication

To have rapport with someone is to be in sync with or on the same wavelength as them. Rapport is established through mutual respect and a genuine interest in another person's opinions, ideas and feelings.

Proficiency in building rapport is fundamental to establishing trusting relationships and greatly facilitates effective communication, collaboration, influence and negotiation.

Nonverbal Communication

Nonverbal communication plays a pivotal role in building rapport. By subtly matching one's body language to the other person, listening, maintaining appropriate eye contact and demonstrating an active engagement, we naturally create a closer contact.

Some examples of non-verbal cues are:

- Connecting through eye contact
- Open-minded and engaged listening
- Forward posture, leaning in to the conversation
- Open gestures (as opposed to closed)
- Voice tone

Other Useful Tips

- Where appropriate, make reference to what the other person has said.
- Say the other person's name from time to time to make them feel acknowledged.
- Remember something specific about the other person for future encounters (their favourite pastimes, children's names, pets)

Internal Assumptions about Rapport[10]

When seeking to build rapport with someone, it can be beneficial to check in with one's internal assumptions to ensure they are aligned with what we are seeking to accomplish.

Below are examples of assumptions that help facilitate a positive and productive mindset:

- *There is always a bridge* (there's always something we have in common)
- *Curiosity is key* (show it by asking questions, listening, showing interest through energy and body language)
- *What you assume is what you get* (positive expectations contribute to successful outcomes)
- *Each individual is a culture* (every person has their own distinct cloud)

---

10 From *The Art of Connecting,* Raines & Ewing

Assignment:

1. Think of a person with whom you have good rapport and describe the feelings of interaction with them in as much detail as you can.

_____

_____

2. Who in your work environment is particularly good at building rapport with people? As you observe them, how do they do this?

_____

_____

3. What can you do to improve your ability to build rapport with others?

_____

_____

About Tool 2.6 Rapport

For many, building rapport with people they don't know is neither easy nor straightforward; and it is generally something that extroverts are better at than introverts.

For coachees who struggle and do not feel at ease in striking rapport with new professional contacts, it is usually hard to know where to start to improve this skill. With a few simple guidelines and tips, the coachee can find points that resonate and build a step-by-step strategy that works for them.

Finding role models for skills such as rapport-building can also be both inspiring and insightful, and observing them in action can provide invaluable clues how to quickly and effectively build rapport.

How to use the tool

The coaching should start by seeking to uncover in what way the coachee is struggling and precisely how the prospect of building rapport with new people makes them feel. From there the coaching can move to providing context to the topic and exploring options, using the tool as a reference for possibilities.

As I take a coachee through this tool I will usually also refer back to **Tool 2.1 The Communication Process**, because in order to build rapport one needs to be open and respectful of the other person and their perspectives. Since nonverbal communication plays such a central role in rapport-building, I will also present or refer back to Tool **2.4 Nonverbal Communication** for additional guidance.

To note:

Internal Assumptions about Rapport. What we expect often becomes our reality, therefore it is of great value for the coachee to understand assumptions and beliefs that help nurture an open and curious mindset, such as is listed in the tool. This part of the conversation may uncover deeper belief patterns that are contributing to the discomfort the coachee feels around rapport. If this is the case then I would recommend coaching on these beliefs as they may otherwise remain potential blocking factors in making progress.

Words Matter

2.7 Inclusive Language

Communication

The purpose of inclusive language is to extend respect and consideration to everyone present so they feel accepted, valued and included.

Examples of sound-bites that can be used in larger contexts:

- ✓ *I value and want to hear **your** opinion.*
- ✓ *How might **we** approach this?*
- ✓ ***We** are all in this **together**.*
- ✓ *How can **we** understand each other better?*
- ✓ ***Everyone** has wisdom.*
- ✓ ***We need each other** to succeed.*
- ✓ ***Everyone's input is valuable** and welcome: what are your experiences/thoughts/ideas?*
- ✓ *What options are available to **us**?*
- ✓ *How can **we** solve this **together**?*
- ✓ *How can **we** achieve an outcome **where everybody wins**?*
- ✓ *What can **we** learn from this?*
- ✓ *Where do **we** go from here?*
- ✓ *This is **our** success.*

Reflection Point:

1. **When would it be useful for you to use inclusive language?**

2. **What are other inclusive sound-bites or phrases that would be applicable in your environment?**

About Tool 2.7 Inclusive Language

It is well established how important diversity is to ensure the high performance, value creation and growth so desperately needed to succeed in today's business environment. The fact that we are all different - that our perspectives, competencies and skills differ - therein lies the value of diversity.

However, it is also vital to recognise that simply promoting diversity and having a varied mix of people does not guarantee high performance (I sometimes see this in Luxembourg where most companies clearly tick the diversity box). High performance requires a culture of *inclusion*, which in turn requires *inclusive leadership*. Diversity will only be a game-changer where there is inclusion.

We are inclusive when everyone in the team or in the room feels respected and treated fairly. We are inclusive when we are open to working together and consider each person's perspective and contribution - when we consciously seek to leverage the group wisdom and create work environments that are *psychologically safe*.

In this context the words we use matter greatly. Using inclusive language helps to build rapport and strengthen relationships between individuals and within teams. It is an effective means to positively influence, create buy-in, inspire engagement and cultivate cultures where people feel they belong.

This is an area where most executives in leadership positions can improve!

How to use the tool

Since most leaders are not used to communicating in an inclusive way, this tool gives examples phrased as sound-bites to encourage coachees to engage in inclusive conversations and to come up with inclusive sound-bites themselves.

When coachees understand and experience the impact of inclusive language, they often become motivated to integrate it into their communication. Those coachees will take the opportunity to work on and rehearse inclusive communication in the safe space that the coaching provides.

"You gain strength, courage and confidence by every experience in which you really stop to look fear in the face. You must do the thing you think you cannot do."

Eleanor Roosevelt

2.8 Assertiveness

Communication

To communicate assertively means having the ability to confidently and clearly share one's opinions, feedback and expectations, while at the same time being open and respectful to the perspectives of others. Being assertive also means setting boundaries when necessary, for example saying no to a request.

In a nutshell, assertive communication:
- Promotes open and honest dialogue without experiencing anxiety or guilt and without violating the dignity of others.
- Increases chances of being understood and thereby getting your needs met.
- Protects you from being taken advantage of by others.
- Encourages initiative and decision-taking.
- Helps to boost self-confidence.

To understand assertiveness, it can be useful to note its position between submission and aggression on what is referred to as the *submission-assertion-aggression continuum*:

Submissive Communication	Assertive Communication	Aggressive Communication

While we may choose to engage in assertive behaviour the majority of the time, there are occasions when the other two behaviours may be more appropriate. Understanding that all three options are available to us, we can choose which one to adopt in any given situation.

Most of us know how to be assertive in some situations in our lives, therefore becoming *more* assertive is usually not about developing a new skill, but rather about applying the existing one in a wider context.

Please reflect on these questions and write your answers in a separate note:

1. **What are some situations in your professional life when it would be beneficial to be more assertive?**

2. **What has blocked you from being assertive in these situations?**

3. **Who do you know who is good at being assertive? As you observe them, what do they do when they are being assertive?**

4. **What concrete steps could you take to improve your assertiveness?**

About Tool 2.8 Assertiveness

Being assertive is an essential communication skill. It enables you to express yourself clearly, stand up for your point of view and set boundaries. This in turn helps to increase self-confidence and earn respect. Because assertiveness is based on respect for others and their rights, it is also an effective way of communicating diplomatically.

Some people are naturally assertive, but for many, speaking up in particular situations can be such a challenge that it can be overwhelming. Typical examples are when participating in certain meetings, when in the presence of senior executives, when giving feedback to someone or when simply saying no.

We can learn to become more assertive in situations we find difficult by practising regularly, starting with small steps and building our confidence as we go along.

How to use the tool

When coaching on this topic I find that many coachees do not fully understand the definition of assertiveness - that it includes the 'respect for others' element. This often results in confusion between *assertiveness* and *aggression*. People typically shy away from being *assertive* because they are afraid that they will appear *aggressive*. I was therefore delighted when I came across the submission-assertion-aggression continuum, where assertiveness is clearly positioned in relation to submission and aggression.

I use this tool to clarify the definition of assertiveness and to introduce the submission-assertion-aggression continuum. The aim of the coaching conversation is to understand in which circumstances the coachee is feeling challenged in being assertive and to work to shift this. The questions that the coachee completes as homework give a good basis to work on.

To note:

The fact that the majority of us know how to be assertive in *some parts of our lives* is frequently overlooked and something few people have even considered. We may find it hard to be assertive at work but have no problem at all being assertive with our child, spouse or parent. I ask the coachee to think about those people or situations in relation to them and ask them to tune into that assertiveness state. From there the coaching can move to how the coachee might duplicate this skill that they already possess in other selected situations.

Sometimes a coachee's lack of assertiveness stems from certain deep-rooted beliefs which make it particularly difficult for them to be assertive. If this is the case then the coaching needs to be focused around helping the coachee unblock these.

"So please ask yourself: What would I do if I weren't afraid? And then go do it."

Sheryl Sandberg

2.9 Communicating Assertively

Communication

Below are some useful tips for assertive communication:

"I" Statements

"I" statements are brief and concise. They allow others to clearly understand what you think and/or feel and thus help remove any ambiguity.

- ✓ "I would like to......."
- ✓ "I choose.........."
- ✓ "I feel......"
- ✓ "I need....."
- ✓ "I do not agree that...."
- ✓ "I would prefer......"
- ✓ "I feel frustrated when...."

Expressing an Opinion

Because everyone has their own point of view, when expressing an opinion it is constructive to the conversation to make clear that this is *your* opinion. Doing so also helps to distinguish between *opinion* and *fact*.

- ✓ "In my opinion......."
- ✓ "It is my experience......"
- ✓ "I understand the situation to be......"
- ✓ "As I see it......"

Saying "No"

The word 'no' is so important and yet many of us find it challenging to say at times. In a work context, learning to say no is critical: you simply cannot be productive if you take on too many commitments. You end up spreading yourself too thin, risk missing deadlines and deliver low quality work. Saying no is one of the most effective ways of setting boundaries. When this is done in a resolute but kind and respectful manner, and with a clear explanation as to why you are saying no, the other party will usually accept your position.

Nonverbal Communication

For a successful outcome, we also need to be congruent in our nonverbal communication and pay attention to:
- Open and receptive body language
- Confident posture
- Steady and calm voice
- Maintaining eye contact
- Open-minded and engaged listening

Practise, Practise, Practise...

About Tool 2.9 Communicating Assertively

Since there is often anxiety and stress around communicating assertively, it is helpful to have access to some different sound-bites as a starting point for the rest of the message.

If giving difficult feedback is part of the assertiveness conversation, then I refer to the **Three-Part Message** in **Tools 1.17 and 1.18**.

How to use the tool

When going through this list of tips with the coachee, I usually ask them to go back to recent experiences where they would have wanted to be more assertive and think about how they could have formulated better sentences. This provides a good opportunity for the coachee to try some of the sound-bites out loud. Doing this often helps to de-dramatise the situation and thereby relieve tension. Realising how simple this is through practice, it is not unusual for the coachee to end up asking themselves what the big deal is. This breakthrough is great to boost confidence and to continue practising with colleagues.

Again, I will always stress the importance of preparation where possible ahead of meetings and for any important conversations.

"Communication - the human connection - is the key to personal and career success."

Paul J. Meyer

2.10 Useful Assumptions about Communication

Communication

Below are some useful assumptions that can help us acquire a more open and flexible mindset when communicating with others:

✓ *People create their own reality based on values, beliefs and the totality of their life experiences.*

✓ *Each person has their unique map of reality (their cloud) and will typically respond to their map, not to reality itself.*

✓ *Words have different meanings for different people.*

✓ *People hear through their own filters (needs, wants, experiences) which may distort the actual message.*

✓ *People often 'code' their messages rather than be direct in their communication.*

✓ *People do the best they can, given the choices they believe are available to them.*

✓ *The vast majority of behaviours have a positive intention, so it can be useful to give others the benefit of the doubt.*

✓ *Communication is both verbal and nonverbal, therefore we are always communicating.*

✓ *Communication is greatly influenced by perception.*

✓ *You have not been effective in your communication until you know that the other person has heard you correctly and understood what you really mean.*

✓ *It is easier to change yourself than to change others.*

About Tool 2.10 Useful Assumptions about Communication

The assumptions we hold will determine how we approach different aspects of our lives. When I studied Neuro-Linguistic Programming (NLP), part of the curriculum included a large set of assumptions to serve as guidelines for operating more smoothly and effectively in this world. If you consciously seek to integrate these guidelines into your mindset, then your journey through life and interactions with others will be more enriching.

This of course also includes the assumptions we hold about communication. I have listed these types of assumptions because they are helpful when thinking about communication from a bigger picture perspective.

How to use the tool

This is a tool that I may give to a coachee in closing the coaching around communication. I find it nicely wraps up the conversations and work done on this topic, and may serve as a useful reminder for the coachee.

Emotional Intelligence

"Emotional intelligence counts more than IQ or expertise for determining who excels at a job... and for outstanding leadership it counts for almost everything."

Daniel Goleman

About Emotional Intelligence

Emotions are central to the human experience. Some emotional intelligence experts claim that we have over 400 emotional experiences every day! Emotions happen instantaneously before we have a chance to think logically about them. Understanding and learning to manage them is what emotional intelligence (EI) is all about.

EI is the ability to:

   ✓ *Identify, understand, and manage your own emotions constructively.*

   ✓ *Recognise and interpret the emotional states of others.*

   ✓ *Connect and engage in such a way that others want to interact and collaborate with you.*

When we interact with others, emotional transactions are taking place - and emotions are infectious. This is why EI is key to forming and developing meaningful and fruitful relationships. When we understand ourselves and others better we can be more conscious in choosing our responses. An emotionally intelligent person will take note of how people around them are feeling and consider this when interacting with them. They will be mindful about their own behaviour to ensure they do not unnecessarily upset or hurt others.

As with most things, some of us are naturally more emotionally intelligent than others. However, none of us is emotionally intelligent 100% of the time: we can all be emotionally hijacked by certain triggers, situations and/or people. The primitive part of our brain is wired to protect and keep us alive, so if a situation is perceived as threatening or unsafe it can result in emotional overwhelm that impedes rational thinking and leads us to react in ways we may later regret. With increased awareness of both self and others, we can learn to consciously pause, achieve mental clarity and change unwanted disruptive emotional responses that may not be helpful. We can learn to manage ourselves and our relationships more intelligently.

EI is not about suppressing emotions or fundamentally changing who we are. EI is about replacing less productive behaviours and learning to channel our emotions in ways that benefit ourselves and others. It is about personal growth, making better decisions and expanding our behavioural repertoire to have more choices available to us in any given situation. As such, EI is a skill (not a condition) that we can continuously develop in order to become increasingly emotionally literate.

The connections we make with others are important: we need each other to do well and lead meaningful lives, be it privately or professionally, and developing EI encourages many positive traits. Popular areas in coaching where people want to improve their EI can range from increasing their level of empathy to communicating more effectively; from managing difficult conversations to developing a leadership style that is inspirational, trustworthy and inclusive.

Given that emotions are such a central part of the human experience, it is interesting to note how much effort has been (and is still being) put into suppressing them, neglecting them and labelling them as a weakness. Strangely, they remain an uncomfortable topic across many parts of our society - including in most organisations.

The Progress Principle, a major study examining the role of emotions in the context of employee engagement[11], proves that emotions directly impact the quality of work and are indispensable to an engaged workforce. This is hardly a surprise when we consider that today's knowledge workers are looking for purpose, meaning and fulfilment at work - aspects strongly related to emotions and personal identity. So if the aim is to foster an engaged workforce who bring their best and whole selves to work, emotions need to be acknowledged.

Once brushed off and even ridiculed, EI is gaining traction in the corporate world and becoming increasingly accepted as a major element in effective leadership. EI experts such as Daniel Goleman maintain that to be truly successful professionally requires one-third IQ (cognitive intelligence) and two-thirds EI; and this increases to 85% at Director and C-levels. This may feel excessive at first glance, but IQ and intellect alone are no longer sufficient: considering that the role of leaders is to inspire, create buy-in, engage and motivate, change will only be possible if followers feel emotionally connected to them. Goleman brings home the point when he states:

"Great leadership works through the emotions."

---

11 Source Amabile and Kramer

"It is very important to understand that emotional intelligence is not the opposite of intelligence, it is not the triumph of heart over head - it is the unique intersection of both."

David Caruso

3.1 EI Model

Emotional Intelligence

Self-awareness is the origin for all conscious change, which is why the upper left quadrant, Emotional Self-Awareness in the EI Model below*, is the starting point for reflecting about yourself and your emotions. Understanding yourself first will help you to better understand those around you.

	SELF	OTHERS
AWARENESS	**Emotional Self-Awareness** *What am I feeling?* *Why am I feeling this way?* (what triggered this emotion)	**Social Awareness** *What are they feeling?* *How can I better understand and value others?* (empathy)
ACTIONS	**Emotional Self-Management** *What do I want to feel?* *How can I manage my emotions so I can be effective ?* (regulate and recover)	**Relationship Management** *How do I want them to feel?* *How do I create constructive and positive work relationships?*

* Daniel Goleman

Clarifying each Quadrant

Emotional Self-Awareness: The ability to recognise your own emotions and how they affect your thoughts, moods, state and behaviour. To have a realistic comprehension of your emotional strengths and weaknesses, and how you come across to those around you.

Emotional Self-Management: The ability to pause in order to control or redirect impulsive or disruptive feelings and behaviours. Achieving emotional balance - learning to manage emotions in a healthy way and adapt to changing circumstances.

Social Awareness: The ability to understand the emotions, needs and concerns of others (empathy). Picking up on emotional cues and recognising the dynamics in interactions with individuals or in a group.

Relationship Management: The ability to develop and maintain good relationships. Lead effectively, communicate clearly, positively influence, collaborate and manage conflict.

Review the EI Model and reflect on the following questions in a professional context.
Insert your answers below each question.

1. How would you describe your emotional self-awareness? (upper left quadrant)

---

2. **What would you say are your emotional strengths and weaknesses?**

_____

_____

3. **What are typical triggers that bring about negative, uncomfortable emotions in you?**

_____

_____

4. **How do you manage your emotions in stressful/conflictual situations?** (lower left quadrant)
   (what you do well and less well)

_____

_____

5. **What are you currently doing to understand the feelings of people around you?** (upper right quadrant)

_____

_____

6. **What do you know about the impact you have on others?** (lower right quadrant)
   (for example the way you communicate and behave)

_____

_____

7. **What are your challenges in applying EI and what would you like to achieve by working on it?**
   (outcomes)

_____

_____

About Tool 3.1 EI Model

This is a fantastic tool for anyone wanting to gain a quick understanding of EI. Each quadrant (and also the model as a whole) gives a good, clear overview that is easy to grasp, making it a great place to start exploring EI.

How to use the tool

I take the coachee through the model, starting with the Emotional Self-Awareness quadrant, followed by Emotional Self-Management, then Social Awareness and finally Relationship Management.

Coaching around the different quadrants will typically generate good initial thinking that is reflective of the coachee's own lived experiences. There is usually enthusiasm around the model as it greatly helps to give structure and context to the abstract topic of EI. The coachee will complete the seven questions as homework for the following session.

To note:

For coachees who have not given much thought to their emotions and triggers, the seven questions can be challenging. This may require quite a bit of gentle probing on the part of the coach, along with patience and compassion to help the coachee dig deeper. However, this work is particularly worthwhile because the insights, understanding and personal breakthroughs are instrumental for developing self-awareness around EI.

"It takes something more than intelligence to act intelligently."

Fyodor Dostoyevsky

3.2 Self-Awareness and Self-Management (EI Model)

Emotional Intelligence

Without conscious awareness we tend to react impulsively and without much consideration when we are triggered in a negative way. With awareness we can learn to pause and calm ourselves to take advantage of our brain's executive centre (prefrontal cortex) which has the capacity to analyse a challenging situation from a broader stance. This executive centre function gives us the freedom to choose the best response.

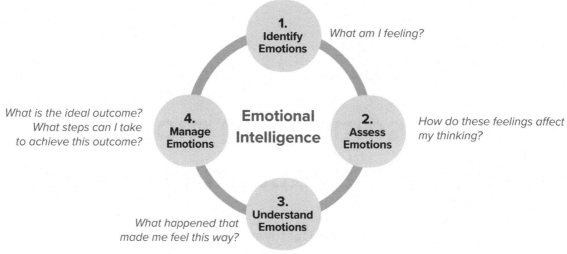

Source: David R. Caruso and Peter Salovey

Here are some simple useful tips to consider when working to improve your EI:

Get curious about your emotional triggers

Stop and consider: why does this person or situation evoke strong negative feelings in you?

Pay attention to how you behave

Notice your behaviour as you experience negative/disruptive emotions. How does it impact your work and overall sense of wellbeing?

Decide how you want to behave

If your response/behaviour in a certain situation is not useful or appropriate, think about how you want to behave instead and what you could do to achieve that.

Take ownership for your emotions and behaviour

If we want to develop our EI, we need to own our emotions and behaviour. Contrary to what we often tell ourselves they are not imposed on us by others: we are responsible for them. This step is often one of the most difficult to accept, but once we do it drowns out a lot of unnecessary inner noise and empowers us to choose our response.

Identify and name your emotions

Without a conscious understanding about what we are feeling it can be hard to manage our emotions and our emotions end up controlling us. Neuroscience reveals that identifying and naming negative/disruptive emotions actually decreases the activity in the amygdala, the part of the brain responsible for activating them, making this a useful strategy for emotional self-management. When we take some distance to investigate and name our emotions accurately we gain better insight into their precise cause. This in turn helps us decide how best to manage them.

Naming emotions can take some reflection as there is a fine yet important distinction between emotions of a similar nature. For instance, "Is it irritation, anger, frustration or annoyance I am feeling?" Or in another situation, "Am I tired, overwhelmed or drained?"

The Emotion Wheel below can be helpful to identify and name emotions.

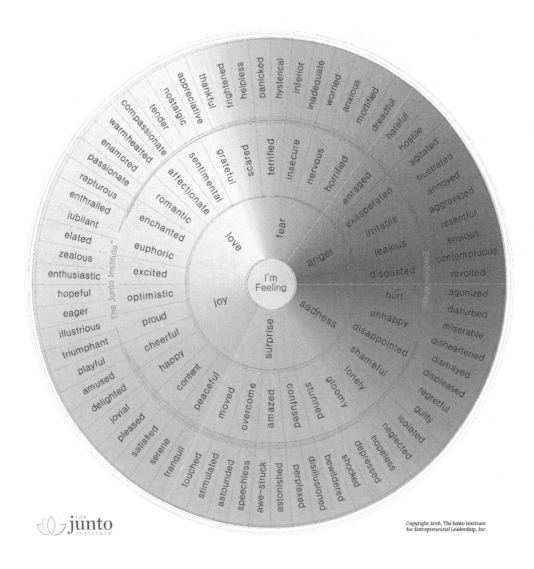

Pause and ask yourself: "What precisely am I feeling?"

Learn to calm yourself

When we are negatively triggered, our body reacts by releasing stress hormones into our system to prepare us to deal with the threat we perceive. These stress hormones will typically make our heart race, increase our blood pressure and make our breathing shallow. As we all know it can be challenging to think clearly in this state as our experience is reduced to a kind of tunnel vision. The best thing to do in this situation (if possible) is to pause, stop talking and focus on calming ourselves to regain clarity.

Contrary to what we may initially believe we *can* learn to calm ourselves, and one of the quickest, simplest and most effective ways to do this is to focus on our breathing. Breathing slowly and deeply from the abdomen decreases the level of the stress hormone cortisol in our system, allowing the strong emotions to reduce in intensity. With practice you can learn to do this quickly and access a more resourceful state. It only takes around ninety seconds for the most stressful neurochemicals to 'rush and flush' through our bodies. However, if the trigger is very strong it is probably best to let more time pass (at least twenty minutes or to sleep on it) before responding.

Understand the difference between Response and Reaction

There is a distinct difference between *responding* and *reacting*. When we experience an emotional trigger, reacting is the unconscious, reflexive and emotional way of addressing the situation. Responding, on the other hand, is a conscious, thoughtful and calm process that involves noticing how you feel, collecting the necessary data about the situation that has triggered you and then *deciding* how you want to behave. Notice how there is ownership in the latter approach: How do I *want* to respond to this?

Challenge your assumptions

Before responding ask yourself: Am I interpreting this correctly? Do I have all the facts? Would it be beneficial to give the other party the benefit of the doubt and verify what they really mean before I decide to get angry?

This step is well worthwhile. We can avoid many unnecessary misunderstandings, tensions and conflicts if we learn to challenge our assumptions more before responding.

Be open to feedback

Being open and receptive to feedback gives us insight about how we are perceived by the people around us; it improves our self-awareness. Feedback can help to uncover potential blind spots and assist us to understand if our behaviour is having the impact we intend.

Practise, practise, practise...

It is not sufficient simply to understand intellectually the concepts of EI: we need to be willing to *practise* our understanding on a regular basis. Developing EI is not a one-off thing, as with most soft skills: it is a lifetime skill that we can keep improving through mindful practice and repetition.

Please reflect and write your answers to the questions below in a separate note:

1. Which of the above points would be particularly useful for you to work on?

_____

_____

2. How and when will you do this?

_____

_____

3. How will you remind yourself and hold yourself accountable?

_____

_____

About Tool 3.2 Self-Awareness and Self-Management

Knowing that we want to improve our EI is easy, but how to actually go about doing this is usually much trickier. Where to begin?

This tool aims to provide coachees with context and tips about how to approach work related to the Self quadrants of the EI Model, in order to better understand their emotional triggers and consider what options are available to them. It also aims to accelerate their learning and creativity around EI, as opposed to the coachees attempting to do this kind of thinking by themselves from a blank page.

How to use the tool

Since the objective is to better understand and manage emotions, the first EI process diagram in the tool is a practical example of what internal questioning and analysis can look like, so spending some time on this diagram is a good way to frame this part of EI.

When it comes to the tips I will usually choose a couple that I know relate particularly to the coachee's situation and coach around these. The coachee will then go through the tool more thoroughly by themselves and answer the last three questions as homework.

The coachee's reflections and answers to the questions provide a good starting point for them to think about strategies for better self-management. However, what seems like a good plan in theory does not always work as well in reality, and it is therefore important that strategies are tried out in practice, as it is normal to want to tweak certain parts as a result of trial and error.

With committed practice progress can be swift, although it is important to remind the coachee that none of us is emotionally intelligent 100% of the time: there are times when we will fall back to an old pattern - and that is all right as long as we are aware, analyse and learn from the events that life hands us. Encouraging the coachee to be patient and compassionate with themselves and acknowledging every success goes a long way to fuel their motivation to keep going.

———————

"I've learned that people will forget what you said, people will forget what you did, but people will never forget how you made them feel."

Maya Angelou

———————

3.3 Reflecting on Real Events

Emotional Intelligence

Think about two separate work-related situations where you were emotionally triggered and would have liked to respond differently. Run each situation through the questions below (use a separate page for each situation).

1. What triggered you to react the way you did?

_____

_____

2. How did you feel? (name the precise emotions)

_____

_____

3. What was the intensity of your emotions? (mark an X on the scale)

CALM   EMOTIONALLY
                                                                     STRESSED

└───┘

4. How did you behave?

_____

_____

5. What do you know about how the other person(s) experienced your behaviour?

_____

_____

6. Were there any other consequences?

_____

_____

With the benefit of hindsight:

7. What would have been a more appropriate level of emotional intensity? (mark a Y on the scale)

_____

_____

8. How would you have liked to respond? What could you have done differently? (please elaborate)

_____

_____

_____

_____

9. **How would you design an alternative strategy (and ultimately a new habit) for similar situations in the future?**

_____

_____

About Tool 3.3 Reflecting on Real Events

Once the coachee has spent time working on the Self aspects of the EI Model, it is beneficial to turn the attention to real life situations.

Exploring past events where it would have been good to handle things differently helps to make reflections more real, advance learning and hardwire useful experiences for future reference. In addition, insights gained from this exercise will help the coachee to build and reinforce better strategies.

How to use the tool

The coachee thinks about two different situations where they would have liked to manage their emotions better. The coaching will then use the questions in the tool as a main guide and with further probing, depending on how things unfold. (To avoid muddled thinking I recommend using a separate sheet for each situation.)

This is a great exercise that brings the coachee's insights to the surface while reliving a past situation and thinking out loud. With the benefit of distance and calm, it is usually easy to access inner wisdom. Strategies formulated in **Tool 3.2 Self-Awareness and Self-Management** will typically be developed and strengthened further as a result of this work.

If the coachee wishes to explore more situations then I will invite them to complete these as homework to be analysed in a next session.

"Empathy is about finding echoes of another in yourself."

Moshin Hamid

3.4 Empathy

Emotional Intelligence

Empathy is seeking to feel what another person is feeling from their perspective, their reality (Social Awareness). Empathy is accessed through our hearts, not our heads, meaning that we first need to connect to our own emotions before can we truly connect to what another is feeling. Developing our ability to empathise is fundamental to building trusting relationships and leading effectively.

Extending empathy doesn't mean that you necessarily have to agree with the other person or their actions. Rather, by attempting to understand them and their position you enable a more compassionate and effective communication and interaction (Relationship Management).

Empathy is a central part of emotional intelligence and a skill that we can nurture and grow throughout our lives. *So how do we go about expanding our empathetic potential?*

Here are some tips:

Listen with the Intention to Understand

Be an exquisite listener. Listen with the *intention to understand* (as opposed to passive hearing). Seek to put yourself in the other person's situation to feel what they are feeling.

Be Caring

Show that you care and acknowledge the other person's feelings and perspective. Paraphrase to ensure that you have understood.

Ask Questions

Be curious, show your interest and ask relevant questions.

Withhold Judgement

Avoid making snap judgements as they tend to shut down the conversation. Give the benefit of the doubt.

Share Vulnerabilities

Empathy is a two-way street, therefore opening up and sharing vulnerabilities goes a long way to creating an emotional connection.

Be open to feedback

Be open to feedback about your level of empathy.

Practise, practise, practise...

Reflect and write your answers in a separate note:

1. In what circumstances would it be beneficial for you to be more empathetic?

2. Which of the tips above would be useful for you to work on with the aim of increasing your level of empathy and why?

3. What immediate opportunity do you have to start practising?

About Tool 3.4 Empathy

Empathy is the most popular aspect of EI that my clients want to develop. Personally, I find this inspiring as it is also one of the qualities that today's employees are looking for in their leaders.

Again, receiving context and tips around empathy is often of great benefit to accelerate learning and progress, as opposed to trying to figure it out by oneself.

How to use the tool

To frame this part I revisit **Tool 3.1 EI Model** as a reminder about where empathy sits in the model. Depending on the coachee/situation, I may also refer to **Tools 2.1 The Communication Process** and **2.5 Levels of Listening**.

To note:

When a coachee is challenged in accessing their empathy, I ask them to think about close relationships with people or pets outside the work environment. Directing attention to loved ones quickly helps to access empathetic emotions. From this place the coaching can return to a professional context where we can address situations when empathy would be beneficial and explore how the coachee can go about developing it.

I go through the tips in the tool with the coachee and ask them to reflect on the three questions as homework, which will serve as points for further discussion in the session that follows.

"When dealing with people, remember you are not dealing with creatures of logic, but with creatures of emotion."

Dale Carnegie

3.5 Meta Mirror

Emotional Intelligence

Reviewing matters from different perspectives in addition to one's own can often bring constructive thinking and empathy to difficult relationship situations. The Meta Mirror[12] technique is a simple but powerful way to obtain invaluable insights into relationship challenges in order to improve and resolve difficult and tense issues.

The technique reviews the same situation from three separate perceptual positions:

1st position - you and your own experience of the relationship

2nd position - viewing the relationship from the other person's perspective

3rd position - observing adequately away from the interaction to access an objective view

Recall an unsatisfactory interaction and exchange with another person.

Process:

1. **Position One**
   Imagine the person in front of you (in position two).
   As you observe them, what are you experiencing, thinking, feeling?
   How do you see the relationship?
   What do you want to say to the other person? (Be exhaustive)

   Break State

2. **Position Two**
   Physically move to position two and imagine that you are the other person.
   (Take on the other person's body language to make it as real as possible)
   As the other person, look at position one. What are you experiencing, thinking, feeling?
   How do you see the relationship?
   How do you respond to what was said to you a few moments ago?

   Break State

---

12 Source: Robert Dilts

3. **Position Three**

   Move to position three and make sure you are dissociated/detached from the situation.

   What are you observing about both parties?

   What are they experiencing?

   What can be learned from this situation?

   What advice would you give to that You in position one?

About Tool 3.5 Meta Mirror

'Going meta' is a Neuro-Linguistic Programming (NLP) term that means stepping away from a situation in order to review it from another viewpoint.

Meta Mirror is a wonderful technique developed by NLP guru Robert Dilts and is primarily used to examine difficult relationship issues. It requires the coachee to physically move from one position/ perspective to the next and spend time reflecting on the same situation in each space. Being in the 2nd and 3rd positions helps bring empathy to the situation and teaches the coachee to dissociate/detach the emotion from the context. This facilitates more constructive and solution-orientated thinking.

From a neuroscience point of view, taking the different physical positions obliges the coachee to access different areas of the brain they would not normally access when thinking about the situation only from their own standpoint. It shows how much more information is available to us when we step out of our own reality - truly fascinating!

While there are five steps in the original technique, many practitioners (including myself) use mostly the first three described here. And because the technique is so effective in bringing empathy to the surface (both for self and others), I will often use it with coachees who want to develop/improve this skill.

How to use the tool

If the coachee describes a situation that could benefit from a Meta Mirror exploration, I will ask if they would like to try out a technique that may help shed light on what is going on. I will then explain the exercise and its different steps. Once the coachee has understood and is keen to try it out, I will ask them to choose where in the room it makes sense to place positions one and two (either sitting or standing). The coachee will usually select the most recent encounter they had with the other person and will often easily choose where to place them.

In each position, I will ask the coachee questions along the lines suggested in the tool. A key for getting the most from the exercise is to encourage the coachee to be fully immersed - to really 'be' in the 1st and 2nd positions. This helps build a complete picture.

Between each step it is important to break state properly. To achieve this I will ask the coachee to physically shake off the previous position and/or jump up and down before entering into the next one.

In the 3rd position there is less emotion, and here it is important that the coachee remains dissociated from the other two positions. Sometimes I will ask the coachee to stand on a chair to really get a different perspective and to ensure that they remain an independent observer.

There is a wealth of information that comes from this exercise, which makes for valuable coaching. I will give the coachee this tool once we have completed the technique so that they also can practise this on themselves, by themselves.

For non-NLP practitioners I would recommend watching videos of this technique (available on the web) to feel more comfortable facilitating yourself or someone else.

Stakeholder Management

"Your network is your net worth."

Porter Gale

About Stakeholder Management

As your career advances and you take on more senior positions, your internal network becomes increasingly important and the support of others becomes critical to your success. The people who have power and/or influence over your role are your *key internal stakeholders*, and they can either support you or block you.

Stakeholder management is the process of proactively building strong and meaningful relationships with these people to obtain their trust, buy-in and support. It is about being visible among powerful and influential colleagues; for them to know you, what you stand for and the value that you bring - your personal brand. Interacting with this group provides valuable opportunities to learn from other seasoned senior executives and engage with them in strategically important conversations.

The coaching centres on helping coachees to think more profoundly about what they want to accomplish by working on this goal: who their key stakeholders are, what their own personal brand is and how they can build and/or strengthen stakeholder relationships in a way that feels comfortable and genuine.

It is not uncommon for people to have reservations about engaging in stakeholder management. Cultural background often plays a part and the most common misgivings range from not being interested in 'playing politics' and preferring to let the work speak for itself, to feelings of not being worthy of senior stakeholders' time and therefore not wanting to disturb them, and not wanting to be perceived as showing off or bragging. However, we are living in an age where the demand on everyone's time is greater than ever. If we fail to get ourselves noticed by our stakeholders and keep them informed (not brag) about important aspects pertaining to the business we manage, the chances are we may be disregarded. If people do not know about you and the value that you bring, you might not get the recognition you deserve and might be overlooked for that next promotion or excluded from that interesting strategic project.

Office politics is part of organisational life. People bring their unique personalities, ambitions, motives and insecurities to work, and politics will often emerge when these differences surface. Alignment is rarely a given. I often highlight that there are two kinds of office politics: the negative self-serving kind, where someone will use whatever means necessary and not care who they negatively impact in the process to advance their agenda (creating mistrust); and the positive value-based kind that seeks to positively influence on topics that are in the best interest of the organisation (inspiring trust). The sooner we accept that politics is part of life at work, we can place our focus on how to navigate ethically within the political lay of the land, because we ignore it at our peril.

Active and deliberate stakeholder management is imperative to lead with impact among the peer group and with superiors, because leading in this context is from a position of influence as opposed to authority. To do this successfully we should be mindful of the crucial role that trust plays in forging strong and lasting professional relationships, attracting sponsors and expanding networks.

This part of the Toolkit focuses solely on *internal* stakeholder management.

"To make progress we have to build a multi-stakeholder process, harnessing the appropriate energies."

Mary Robinson

4.1 Stakeholder/Power Map

Stakeholder Management

Stakeholder/ Power Map

Identify and place each stakeholder on the map:

High Power/ Influence	Strengthen relationships - get on their radar!	Continue to manage closely
Medium	Monitor	Keep informed with regularity
Low Power/ Influence		

Low Interpersonal Closeness   Medium   High Interpersonal Closeness

Reflection point:
What does your completed map tell you?

About Tool 4.1 Stakeholder/Power Map

'Stakeholder mapping' is the process of identifying and placing stakeholders on a grid in accordance with a set of criteria on each axis. There are several stakeholder map templates used for a variety of purposes, one of the most popular being Mendelow's *Power-Interest Matrix*. The map on the previous page is inspired by this matrix, where I have added *Influence* to *Power* and switched the original criterion *Interest* with *Interpersonal Closeness*. I find this set to be more relevant when working on internal stakeholder management.

The Stakeholder/Power Map is a great tool to get a visual overview of the people who have power and/or influence over your role and what you want to achieve. It sheds light on how those people are connected to you and also to each other. Even though the main focus should be placed on the two upper quadrants (High Power/Influence), it is also important to consider key players in the two lower quadrants. Organisations evolve rapidly and people initially placed in a low power quadrant may suddenly move to a high one - something that I regularly witness while working with my clients on this topic. Since stakeholders, power and alliances may change, the map should therefore be reviewed regularly.

How to use the tool

The first step is to identify the stakeholders, who are usually within superior and peer groups. This may require some careful thinking, especially in matrix organisations that operate across borders. It can be helpful for the coachee to verify their list with their manager to ensure good coverage.

The mapping needs to reflect how things *currently* stand. To familiarise the coachee with the exercise I will ask them to identify a few stakeholders and start placing them on the map during the initial coaching session. The coachee will first map their relationship with each stakeholder, and once that has been done I will ask them to consider the relationships *between* the stakeholders: are they supportive of each other or not? It is good to bear in mind that some people have power and influence even though they are not senior in the organisational hierarchy, so "Who influences whom?" A simple example is the executive assistant who may be highly influential because of the close relationship they have with their manager. These three perspectives will influence the coachee's strategies in approaching their different stakeholders.

The coachee completes the map on their own for the following coaching session.

A completed map may look something like this:

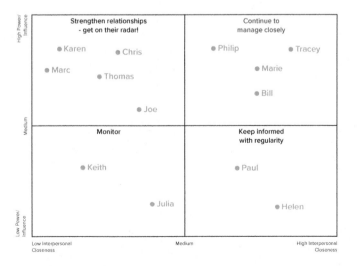

The upper right hand quadrant - the 'sweet spot' - is where you find the potential sponsors. These stakeholders need to be managed closely and should ideally be converted into sponsors if they are not already. Sponsors are powerful people involved in your career who have your back, open doors and actively support you when you are not in the room. Having sponsors is fundamental to grow, advance and enjoy a successful career, and it is the coachee's responsibility to find their sponsors. The upper left quadrant is where the coachee needs to invest: as the map implies, the relationships with these powerful and influential stakeholders are weak or non-existent, so the aim is to move them to the right side of the map.

This is a dynamic tool and the coachee will update the Stakeholder/Power Map as actions are implemented and relationships evolve.

"To keep everyone invested in your vision, you have to back up a little bit and really analyse who the different stakeholders are and what they individually respond to."

Alan Stern

4.2 Stakeholder Analysis

Stakeholder Management

Part 1. What you know about each stakeholder (blue cloud)

Stakeholder	What do you know about the stakeholder's current opinion of you?	Who influences their opinion of you?	How would you describe your current relationship? (interpersonal closeness)	How is your work/ role/ experience of interest to this person? (What do you know about their expectations?)	What information/ knowledge/ resources do you have that could be of benefit to them?	What are potential 'bridges' (common interests, connection points, synergies) between you and the stakeholder that you could use to strengthen the relationship?
<Stakeholder Name>						
<Stakeholder Name>						
<Stakeholder Name>						

Example

Karen	Good with local issues but she doesn't think I am sufficiently involved at regional level	Myself, Philip, Marie & John	She knows who I am but there is not much of a relationship. (I really need to change this)	My ability to contribute to regional efficiencies and to the overall strategic agenda	Internal processes / Client feedback / Key projects	Operational details, efficiencies and improvements. I heard she loves skiing as do I.

Part 2. Important for you (your cloud)

Stakeholder	What specifically do you want this stakeholder to know about you and your world?	How can you ensure that you are relevant to them?	Are your current actions and interactions with this person producing the results you want?	What opportunities do you have (or can you create) to interact more effectively with this person?
<Stakeholder Name>				
<Stakeholder Name>				
<Stakeholder Name>				

Part 3. Clarifying Alignment

Stakeholder	What do you know about the stakeholder's current opinion of you?	What specifically do you want this stakeholder to know about you and your world?	As you compare the two columns to the left, how would you describe the alignment?
<Stakeholder Name>			
<Stakeholder Name>			
<Stakeholder Name>			

About Tool 4.2 Stakeholder Analysis

Once the stakeholders have been identified and placed on the Stakeholder/Power Map, it is useful to conduct an analysis that answers two fundamental questions: *What do I know about each of them?* and *What do I want them to know about me and my world?*

With these two questions in mind I have created a Stakeholder Analysis that prompts deeper thinking about each stakeholder. The more we know about our stakeholders and consider what is important for ourselves in developing those relationships, the stronger position we will be in to define actions that will give impact and accelerate traction.

How to use the tool

Effective stakeholder management is about understanding each stakeholder's 'blue cloud' in order to be relevant and proactively build bridges that lead to meaningful relationships, so I will frame this exercise using **Tool 2.1 The Communication Process** and if relevant **2.6 Rapport**.

The first two parts of the analysis are based on the Communication Process model's clouds:

Part 1: The coachee's current knowledge about each stakeholder (blue cloud)

Part 2: What is important for the coachee in relation to each stakeholder? (green cloud)

Part 3: This addresses alignment. The first columns from parts 1 and 2 are placed next to each other so that the coachee can easily compare their answers and reflect on the current situation outcome.

This is one of the more sizeable exercises in the Toolkit. I will take the coachee through the three parts and ask them to complete the analysis for the following coaching session. The exercise is both insightful and challenging as it becomes clear to the coachee what they know and do not know (fields left blank) about each stakeholder. Becoming clear about what is currently unknown presents an opportunity to find this out. If certain relationships are weak or non-existent, I will encourage the coachee to think of other people who have good relationships with the stakeholders they want to get closer to and ask them for advice and tips to fill out the blanks, find the bridges or open the doors that will help.

Similar to Tool **4.1 Stakeholder/Power Map**, the Stakeholder Analysis is a dynamic tool to be updated as the coachee learns more about each stakeholder.

"You too are a brand. Whether you know it or not. Whether you like it or not."

Marc Ecko

"If you're not branding yourself, you can be sure others do it for you."

Unknown

4.3 Personal Brand

Stakeholder Management

We all have a brand, whether we are aware of it or not. Your personal brand is the perception others have of you when they think about you and talk about you. The impression you make on your colleagues is significant because it determines whether you get recommended, recognised, promoted or assigned the important projects, and whether others want to follow you.

Your personal brand reflects your values, vision, strengths, skills and experience. It reflects your uniqueness and the value that you bring.

When you are clear about your personal brand - how you want to be perceived - it is your responsibility to ensure that it becomes visible to others through your communication, contribution, behaviour and actions.

This prompts the following questions:

1. How would you describe your personal brand? (Be specific)

_____
_____
_____

2. Is it aligned with how you are currently perceived by your stakeholders?
(If not, then what is missing?)

_____
_____
_____

3. How do you want others to talk about you and what do you want them to say?

_____
_____
_____

4. What aspects of your brand do you want to strengthen or visibly demonstrate more of?

_____
_____
_____

Assignment:
Reflect on the above questions and write your answers.

About Tool 4.3 Personal Brand

In today's corporate environment there is an expectation for employees to take ownership and manage their career to proactively move it in the direction they desire. An essential part of this is being mindful about one's personal brand - particularly when in a leadership role. As we have established, your brand determines whether you get recommended, recognised, promoted and assigned the important projects, and last but not least whether others want to follow you.

This tool aims to bring personal branding to the forefront of the coachee's mind and think about what is important for them in how they come across to their colleagues, including their stakeholders.

How to use the tool

In my experience most executives have not given much thought to their personal brand. For many it is not an easy exercise; for some it may even be uncomfortable to think about their brand. The coaching will typically centre on questions such as these to support the coachee in their reflection:

- What is important to you?
- What are your values? Are they visible to others?
- What are you passionate about? What energises you?
- What are your core skills and competencies?
- What are your key accomplishments?
- How are you unique? What is that special thing *you* bring?

Once the coachee is clear about what they want their brand to be, the next step is to think about how to make it visible to others. It is important to drive home the point that if you do not speak up other people will not know what you want or the value that you add; and crucially they may assume that you are not interested - or perhaps not even qualified for that promotion or next great project.

Working on your personal brand is not about making up things about yourself or coming up with some complicated strategy. On the contrary, it is about knowing *who* you are, *what* you represent (your values) and *how* you stand out. It is an opportunity to think about whether you are making the impact you desire.

To note:

Question 4 is often challenging for coachees to answer. High performance alone is not sufficient: trust is also essential to build strong and lasting relationships. The Performance-Trust Matrix made popular by Simon Sinek serves as a good reminder of this and can help spark valuable insights to this question. Talented executives want to be in the green quadrant - so is the coachee there? And if not, what do they need to do (behaviours and actions) to get there?

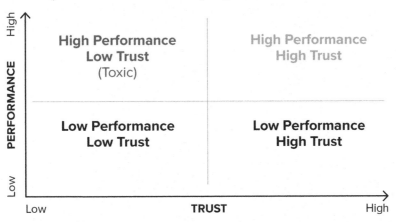

Courage starts with showing up and letting ourselves be seen."

Brené Brown

4.4 Concrete Actions

Stakeholder Management

Review your work

1. Go back to your Power Map and remind yourself where your stakeholders are positioned:
   - Who is in the upper right quadrant (potential sponsors)?
   - Who is in the upper left quadrant (not yet actively supporting you)?

2. Review your Stakeholder Analysis and reflect on your conclusions (all 3 parts).

3. Consider your insights around your Personal Brand.

Assignment:
Consider how you can proactively strengthen and effectively manage these relationships through *engaging, collaborating, supporting, challenging* and *advising*.

Think about what opportunities are *available* to you and what opportunities you can *create*.

Stakeholder	Concrete Actions	Target Date (for each action)

Building meaningful and trusting relationships with your key stakeholders allows you to serve the organisation better, influence how you are perceived, achieve greater impact and accelerate your career.

About Tool 4.4 Concrete Actions

Once the coachee has completed the preparation work of identifying and analysing their stakeholders and gained clarity about their personal brand, it is time to define concrete actions. The actions should be thoughtful and take into account each stakeholder's blue cloud (**Tool 2.1 The Communication Process**).

How to use the tool

Having done the groundwork using the previous tools, the coachee will be eager to move to the action phase. Proactivity will play an important role here: it is not just about what opportunities are already *available* to the coachee, but also what opportunities the coachee can *create*.

Coaching centres around the following points:

- How can you get on your stakeholder's radar? (Upper left quadrant in the power map)
- How will you make interactions relevant and meaningful?
- How will you nurture the relationships in the sweet spot of your power map?
- Do you have the right sponsors to get you to where you want to be?
- How will you go about being impactful? (Personal brand)

I often highlight that reciprocity is a good way to build bridges and strengthen relationships. Reciprocity is the practice of exchanging something with someone else for mutual benefit. When people receive something of value to them, most will naturally feel an obligation to reciprocate, so a good way to start connecting with stakeholders is understanding what is of interest to them (**Tool 4.2 Stakeholder Analysis**). Simple actions can be a good start: sending an executive summary or an article that could be of interest to the stakeholder. Coachees often overlook useful resources they can draw on, including such things as their expertise, experience, network and their time.

It is important to bear in mind that for interactions and exchanges to be *valuable* they should be *bi-directional*, both demonstrating a sincere interest in the stakeholder's world and sharing useful insights into one's own. By paying attention to what people talk about and what they actively involve themselves in, you can often get clues about *what you have* that could be of value to them.

To gain positive momentum and traction in the busy corporate environment, it is important to make stakeholder management a priority and carve out time for actions on a regular basis (ideally weekly).

Influencing and Negotiation

"Unless both sides win, no agreement can be permanent."

Jimmy Carter

About Influencing and Negotiation

Whether introducing a new idea, sourcing additional headcount or seeking increased project budgets, the need to influence and negotiate with relevant stakeholders is very much part of everyday corporate life. Alignment cannot be taken for granted given people's different needs, wants, goals and ambitions. Knowing how to be impactful is extremely valuable, and influencing and negotiating upwards with superiors, sideways with peers and downwards with teams is necessary to keep business priorities moving forward.

Influencing and negotiating are closely linked (although with subtle differences) and the skills required are similar, which is why I have chosen to address them together in the Toolkit. To influence is to be respectful and impactful in bringing others around to seeing things from your perspective. To negotiate is to be able to address an issue with one or more people and reach an agreement that is satisfying to all parties.

Every human interaction is an emotional transaction. Emotions are infectious and our decisions are greatly influenced by them, so to be effective in influencing and negotiating requires the ability to connect to people's emotional centres in a way that creates resonance within them. The mindset and attitude we adopt are central to achieving the best possible outcome, and as with most things we have options: we can choose a self-interested "I win, you lose" mindset or opt for an inclusive bigger-picture win-win mindset.

'Win-win' has become a corporate buzz-phrase and I sometimes feel it is being used without much consideration for the true meaning behind the expression. A win-win approach seeks the mutual benefit of everyone involved in the interaction - to find an outcome where everybody wins. However, because many of us are raised in cultures that favour competition, our natural tendency is the opposite of win-win: to pursue our own interest and defend our position with a mindset that says "It's either my way or your way" - ie win-lose. Those operating with a win-lose mindset do so with the combative belief that in order to win, another person has to lose. Although we may achieve certain gains using the win-lose approach, we also run the risk of creating low trust and resentment with the people we work with, and therefore those gains may be short-lived.

Clearly it may not always be possible or practical to go for win-win in every situation: there will be times when compromise or win-lose are the best options. However, we can certainly *intend* to have a win-win mindset as a starting point for collaborating, influencing and negotiating with others - because we all prefer to interact with someone who has the bigger picture in mind and everyone's best interest at heart.

Being conscious of one's mindset and open to a win-win whenever possible makes for trustful working relationships. This in turn leads to quicker and better outcomes, creativity, synergies and innovation that ultimately benefit the organisation as a whole.

"Win-win is a belief in the Third Alternative. It's not your way or my way; it's a better way, a higher way."

Stephen Covey

5.1 Win-Win Mindset

Influencing and Negotiation

Having a win-win mindset is to:

✓ *Believe that there is sufficient for everyone (abundance vs scarcity thinking)*

✓ *Believe that opportunities are limitless*

✓ *Proactively invest in building trustful and collaborative (rather than competitive) relationships*

✓ *Create conditions where everyone in the interaction can experience a win*

✓ *Demonstrate openness and listen with the intention to really understand*

✓ *Have the courage to express one's own views and seek to be understood*

✓ *Be respectful, inclusive and considerate of everyone*

✓ *Take care that all parties feel good and are committed to the solution/outcome*

✓ *Understand that it is not necessarily "my way, your way or no way" but that there may be a better way worth exploring*

About Tool 5.1 Win-Win Mindset

A win-win mindset operates from the assumption that there is enough for everyone, without feelings of scarcity. Coming to the table with a vantage point of infinite possibilities will inspire others to engage in collaborative thinking and motivate them to work with you, thereby increasing your chance to successfully influence and negotiate.

Because thinking win-win does not come naturally to many of us, this tool helps the coachee to grasp the underlying beliefs that underpin a win-win mindset. Understanding these beliefs is necessary to consciously integrate them into one's way of thinking and operating, and to know that with awareness and practice we can adopt a win-win mindset.

How to use the tool

At the very outset of working on Influencing and Negotiation I usually frame the coaching conversation in line with the introductory *About* section and spend time learning where the coachee is coming from in wanting to work on this topic. We then explore how the concept of win-win and the points in the tool relate to the coachee.

To note:

To raise awareness it is sometimes helpful to get the coachee to consider what kind of people they like to work with: is this someone who is *closed to the opinions of others* and primarily focused on their own interests or someone who is *open to listen and consider the opinions and ideas of others*? Thinking about influencing and negotiation from this angle and what that says about the coachee's personal brand usually brings great insight.

"There are three ways of dealing with difference: domination, compromise, and integration. By domination only one side gets what it wants; by compromise neither side gets what it wants; by integration we find a way by which both sides may get what they wish."

Mary Parker Follett

5.2 Six-Step Strategy

Influencing and Negotiation

1. Think about your aims
- What is your desired outcome?
- What is your intention? (win-win or win-lose)
- What options could result in win-win?
- How does your proposal add value to the overall strategy and/or the organisation?

2. Consider the other person(s):
- What do you know about them?
- What do you know about their situation and their desired outcome?
- What arguments are they most likely to have?
- Are you bringing options and solutions that would also benefit them?

3. Prepare your delivery
- Where possible prepare in advance.
- Consider how you will communicate your case given what you know about the other parties.
- To safeguard relationships focus on your respective needs and interests (instead of positions).
- Clarify how your proposal fits into the bigger picture perspective.

4. Establish rapport and listen
- Extend your respect and genuine willingness to establish a good rapport.
- Listen at the highest level. Ask questions and paraphrase to ensure you really understand the other person's situation.

Listening at the highest level can provide you with valuable insights and thereby increase your chances to influence. Influence is a two-way consideration: you must yourself be open to influence in order to influence others.

5. Present your case
- Present your case with clarity and in a way that aims to resonate with the other party.
- Base your reasoning on facts and evidence.
- Seek to incorporate the areas that are important to both sides, including what you have just learned by listening.

6. Negotiate with win-win in mind
- When all parties understand one another, aim to negotiate for outcomes that are beneficial for everyone.

About Tool 5.2 Six-Step Strategy

To develop and improve one's skillset in this domain, it is useful to have a structure, and as you might expect there are several methods/models for influencing and negotiation. I have developed the collaborative six-step approach here around the overriding inclusive spirit of this tool book.

Once we move away from win-lose to consciously integrate a win-win way of thinking and operating, there is truly no limit to what we can achieve together. When influencing and negotiation are approached from this stance we create a level playing field and a psychologically safe environment that enables mutual exploration, curiosity and collaboration, instead of a stressful, tense and combative setting.

The steps for *influencing* and *negotiation* are the same up to the sixth and final step, negotiating a mutually satisfactory outcome.

If a coachee's role demands them to be particularly skilful in the art of negotiation, I will recommend that they enrol in a training course focused on this, and bring learnings and take-aways into the coaching sessions for practice, fine-tuning and integration.

How to use the tool

To keep things real I ask the coachee to bring one or more upcoming situations to the coaching sessions and work on these using the six-step strategy.

The preparation required in points 1, 2 and 3 are of particular importance because taking the time to reflect and work through them will greatly increase the chance of success. I (re-)introduce **Tool 2.1. The Communication Process**, to remind the coachee about the value of taking the other person(s) and their cloud(s) into account. To view the same situation from several perspectives helps to dissociate emotionally from our own standpoint and see things as a whole. From this bigger picture view we are able to access greater insights and options in order to have the desired impact to influence and negotiate.

To note:

For point 2, **Tool 2.2 Perception** can be a good complement to **Tool 2.1 The Communication Process** in highlighting the value of considering different perspectives. The sooner we learn to accept each other's viewpoints, the more readily we will be able to constructively brainstorm a way forward that works for all parties.

For point 4, I may refer to **Tools 2.5 Levels of Listening** and **2.6 Rapport** for additional guidance and support. Listening at the highest level provides the opportunity to collect valuable information about the other person's situation as well as test whether initial assumptions are in fact correct. Paraphrasing one's understanding of what the speaker is trying to convey further demonstrates a willingness to fully understand where they are coming from. By listening first you are better equipped to make your case; and because you have listened at the highest level, chances are that your counterpart(s) will extend the same level of listening when it is your turn to speak.

For point 5, to deliver with intended impact I often recommend that the coachee write down *how* they plan to present their case and then rehearse it by themselves and/or in the coaching session. Rehearsing is a useful means to validate and fine-tune, both from a verbal and nonverbal standpoint.

Personal Efficiency and Effectiveness

"Until we can manage time, we can manage nothing else."

Peter Drucker

About Personal Efficiency and Effectiveness

Time may be the only resource where we are all truly equal. No one has more than twenty-four hours in their day and the demands on this limited resource are now greater than ever. It is no surprise that personal efficiency and effectiveness in the context of time and priority management is a popular coaching topic.

In the corporate world business transformation and change have become the new constants, and time and priority management are essential to navigate today's complex bureaucratic work environments. In most companies, 'business as usual' (BAU) has evolved to such an extent that people are being inundated by countless issues, emails, back-to-back meetings and unexpectedly 'urgent' tasks. Unfortunately this BAU mode frequently takes precedence over important business aspects, such as allocating enough time to think about strategic matters, planning for the longer term and creating the space required for employees to be creative and innovate. And even if these important aspects do get scheduled into already overloaded calendars, they are far too often cancelled or abridged, and replaced by urgent tasks and sometimes even guilt on the part of executives - since taking the time to think makes many people feel unproductive. Corporate world has become obsessed with activity to the point that we rarely stop and think about what we are busy with - or if it even makes sense - leaving people feeling overwhelmed in what is perceived as an ever faster-spinning hamster wheel.

It is not uncommon to reach the end of a busy working day and feel frustrated about not having achieved much. This feeling usually stems from being insufficiently focused on one's priorities, and rather working on tasks that should be delegated, spending too much time in firefighting mode, attending unnecessary meetings, being distracted by electronic devices and getting pulled into other people's agendas/priorities. Days are easily filled with *busyness* but without adequate attention to getting the right *business* things done.

Prioritisation has therefore become an essential leadership skill: no single person can be involved in everything and be constantly available to everyone. Leaders need to prioritise, manage their time and delegate to lead successfully. To do this they must first become clear about what is expected from them in their role. Priorities can only be defined when there is an understanding about how one's performance will be measured and evaluated. Once this clarity has been achieved, having a solid personal organisation maintained through regular planning is crucial to ensure attention is placed on the right priorities and with minimal waste of time.

There is often confusion between being *efficient* and being *effective*. A simple way to distinguish between the two is that *efficiency* is about doing things in an optimised way with minimum expense or effort (working smarter), while *effectiveness* is doing the right things (working on priorities) - and both are required to be productive and perform well.

Only by being organised, self-disciplined and in control of the workload is it possible to manage time and prioritise, effectively lead others, keep commitments to colleagues and clients and meet deadlines. Developing an efficient approach to managing professional commitments does more than just make you more effective and productive: it also gives you more time and opportunity to create a balanced life.

"The key is not to prioritise what's on your schedule, but to schedule your priorities."

Stephen Covey

6.1 Eisenhower Matrix

Personal Efficiency and Effectiveness

Eisenhower Matrix

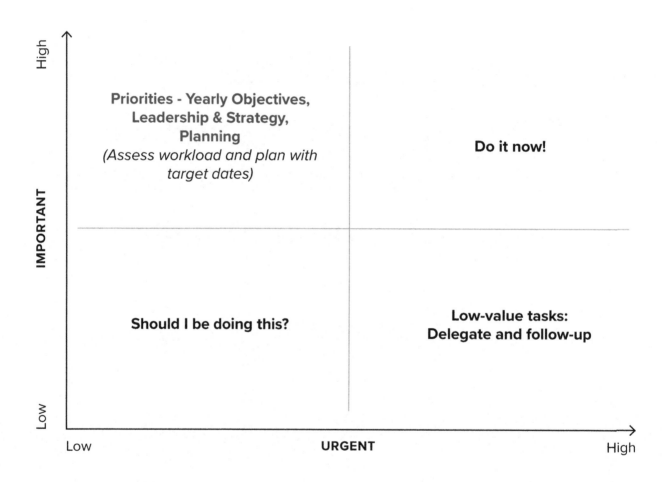

About Tool 6.1 Eisenhower Matrix

Prior to becoming the 34th President of the United States of America, Dwight D. Eisenhower served in the US army as a five-star general during World War II. Being required to make tough decisions on a continual basis, he recognised the benefit of differentiating between what was important and what was urgent, and to organise his work accordingly. Eisenhower was cognisant that successful time management is about being effective as well as efficient: that time needs to be spent on important tasks and not just the urgent ones.

The Eisenhower Matrix, through its aerial perspective, helps to prioritise workload by clarifying which activities and tasks are important rather than urgent. With this clarification, unimportant but urgent tasks can be delegated and the time gained used on the important tasks required to be effective and successful. I am a big fan of the Eisenhower Matrix for its simple and comprehensive application, which extends beyond business: it is a great tool that can be used in all areas of life to prioritise and plan.

How to use the tool

Most executives I work with are familiar with the Eisenhower Matrix and have come across it in previous corporate trainings. As I re-introduce it I ask in which of the four quadrants they are spending most of their time in an average day/week. Many will conclude that they spend too much time in the *Urgent High* quadrants and far too often in firefighting mode. When asked if *where* they are spending their time matches *what* they are seeking to achieve (their priorities and vision), the answer will usually be no as they sit back in quiet reflection contemplating the Matrix.

The Matrix is used from the perspective of a person's *role*, meaning that when thinking about the importance of tasks and responsibilities these should be assessed in relation to the expectations of that role. The tasks in the *Important Low/Urgent High* quadrant are considered low value in relation to the coachee's role, and should therefore be delegated for the coachee to operate at their appropriate level. However, it is not uncommon for people to spend too much time in this quadrant instead of delegating. The most common reasons for this are that the person is not prioritising their work, the low value tasks are in their comfort zone, they do not trust others to execute tasks well and believe they are the only one capable of doing them, or a lack of resources.

The objective of the coaching is to raise the coachee's awareness about the importance of operating from the top two *Important High* quadrants: working on the tasks and responsibilities that will enable them to be successful in their role. Of these quadrants, the majority of time should be spent in *Important High/Urgent Low:* working on priorities, actively leading, planning and engaging in strategic thinking (thus minimising time in the high adrenaline *Urgent High* quadrant). Spending sufficient time in this quadrant is necessary to be effective and this is accomplished by being organised and planning ahead.

To adopt better habits around prioritisation I encourage coachees to frequently ask themselves: *In my role, should I be doing this? If not then who should be and/or where does this task belong?* And to regularly challenge the status quo with *Should we still be doing this?* or *Is this a waste of time?* or *Can it be done better?*

In addition to using the Matrix on themselves, I also frequently encourage coachees to use it with their teams to prioritise and plan the overall team workload.

"You can do anything, but not everything"

David Allen

6.2 Checkpoint

Personal Efficiency and Effectiveness

Please answer the following questions:

Eisenhower Matrix (aerial view)
- In what quadrants are you typically spending the majority of your time?
- Does your current way of operating match your intention? What you are seeking to achieve?

Your Work Priorities (the things expected from your role)
- List your top work priorities and be specific (Important High Quadrant):
- Does your weekly and daily planning reflect your priorities?

Planning the Workload (getting focused and (re)gaining control)

Weekly
- How are you currently planning your workload?
- What makes most sense: to plan one or two weeks ahead?
- What is the best day and time each week for you to work on your weekly planning?

Daily
- How do you plan your daily tasks and priorities?
- What is working well and what not so well?

Clearing the Disorder (creating space)
- Describe the current status of your electronic mailbox.
- Describe the current status of your paperwork and paper organisation.
- What are some concrete actions you can take to create space (electronic and paper)?

Your Commitment
- On a scale 1 to 5 (5 = highest) how committed are you to achieving this coaching goal and why?

Additional Points
- Is there anything else that would help you become more organised, efficient and effective?

About Tool 6.2 Checkpoint

This tool builds on the coachee's insights from **Tool 6.1 Eisenhower Matrix**. Since perception and reality are rarely aligned when it comes to priority and time management, the purpose of this tool is to give the coachee and the coach an accurate picture of how they are currently organising themselves. It is only possible to identify appropriate actions if there is a good understanding about what is actually going on. The tool takes the coachee through a top-down approach, starting from an aerial perspective and then drilling down to cover work priorities and personal organisation.

How to use the tool

In framing this part I point out that personal organisation is similar to ensuring a strong foundation before building a beautiful house: if the foundation is weak, it will not support the house. In completing the questions in the tool it quickly becomes clear where the pain points are. The coaching focuses on creating a structure that works for the coachee to get organised and take themselves to the top two quadrants of the Eisenhower Matrix.

To note:

Work Priorities. I always spend time on the priorities that the coachee has identified to ensure the list is complete and accurately reflects the expectations of their role. It is not uncommon for a few priorities to have been left out and/or for one or two to have been included that do not belong in the list.

Planning the Workload. To be in control of workload, planning needs to be conducted weekly and daily to have a good overview and to focus consistent attention on priorities. In my experience most people tend to overestimate the time they have available and/or underestimate how long it takes to complete different tasks: they are *time-optimistic*. Activities and tasks that require focused attention need to be blocked in the calendar and given realistic time slots. Being *time-realistic* makes it easier to plan and to protect oneself from too many distractions. The amount of time that emails, calls, unexpected tasks and 'quick' questions take up is often underestimated, and this also needs to be anticipated and taken into account.

Meetings have spun out of control in the corporate environment. They take up well over 50% of workers' time and are regularly scheduled back-to-back, leaving no time to prepare. They are also often poorly run and without proper consideration about who actually needs to be present. Because every wasteful meeting takes time away from priority work, I ask the coachee to make a review of the meetings they are invited to and consider whether they really need to attend or if there are some they can delegate.

Clearing the Disorder. A clear and focused mind is supported by keeping work tools and documents in good order. I often compare this to cooking: no matter how great the ingredients, if your kitchen is not shipshape you will first need to clean it up if you want to pull off that great meal.

Similar to meetings, emails are a huge problem. Most people receive anything from fifty to several hundred emails per day. This can result in feelings of overwhelm as it is just not possible to effectively process so much correspondence in addition to everything else that needs to be done. As a first step I ask the coachee to sift through their inbox to verify if they really need to receive all the mails they receive and to unsubscribe themselves from anything irrelevant to them. With the current email situation having such a negative impact on employees, their wellbeing and general productivity, I am surprised that so few organisations have implemented email etiquette rules!

>>

Additional Points. The answer to the final question in the tool is often *procrastination.* Procrastination is a trap most of us fall into at one time or another. However, for some people it can be a real issue with serious consequences, such as consistently missing deadlines, failing to deliver on commitments or causing others not to want to work with them. It is useful to know that procrastination is a *conscious* action whereby we *choose* to do something else other than the task in hand; and this usually involves disregarding important tasks that have an unpleasant component to them in favour of tasks that are easier or more enjoyable.

In the first instance, the coaching seeks to shed light on *why* the coachee is procrastinating: is it lack of organisation, avoidance of tasks perceived as tedious, a sense of overwhelm, perfectionism or a lack of confidence? Understanding the root cause is important to identify relevant strategies and actions that will help the coachee overcome their procrastination and adopt better habits.

"If you want to do a few small things right, do them yourself. If you want to do great things and make a big impact, learn to delegate."

John C. Maxwell

6.3 Effective Delegation

Personal Efficiency and Effectiveness

Effective delegation is a thoughtful process that takes into account the assignment to be delegated as well as the individual's skills, interest and development needs. Not all tasks (such as routine tasks) need to be thoroughly considered; but when it comes to important tasks and assignments, putting them into an appropriate context and clarifying expectations makes a notable difference.

Here are some useful points to consider when delegating tasks and responsibilities:

Delegate to operate at your level

Focus on the quadrants *Important High* (Eisenhower Matrix) for your role and delegate the rest with the aim for you to operate at your level and increasingly achieve results through your team members. The more senior your role is, the more you need to be reviewing, supporting, challenging, coaching and mentoring instead of executing on low-value tasks. This approach is required to take yourself and your team to a level of high performance.

Take some time and reflect on your entire workload. Use the Eisenhower Matrix to help you assess what you should be focusing on yourself and what you should be delegating. Consider the long-term perspective: is executing that particular task a good use of your time? How will you benefit in the longer run if you delegate it?

Delegate to develop and empower team members

An essential objective of delegation is to enable your team members to grow professionally, so make sure to include both challenging and routine tasks. To strengthen their empowerment aim to delegate complete assignments for which they can be responsible. Ask how they would like to be supported and how they would like to report on progress (rather than you instructing these).

Promote autonomy by asking questions such as:

"Now that you are clear about the outcomes, what is your plan?"

"What kind of support would you like from me in order to be successful?"

Be clear about purpose and expectations

Begin with the end in mind. Explain why the task you are delegating is important and what purpose it serves and seek to connect it to the bigger picture. When people understand why they have been asked to do something they are far more likely to assume ownership of the assignment.

Be clear about what you expect in terms of priorities, quality, format, outcomes and target dates. Ensure that team members understand your expectations. If you are uncertain, ask them to paraphrase their understanding of your expectations.

Remember, *nothing goes without saying and nothing is obvious*.

References of 'best practice' work

In some cases it can be highly useful to find pieces of work that well reflect the level of quality you are looking for. Show these to your team members and explain why they meet your expectations so that your team have good points of reference.

Focus on the results

To avoid micro-managing, focus should be on results and the 'big lines'.

Accept mistakes

Accept that mistakes will be made and that it is important for people to be allowed to do this as part of their learning process. When mistakes happen, review together with the team member and ensure that learning has taken place so that the same mistake is not repeated. Learn to live with differences, because as individuals we are all different and it is not your mission to transform your team members into replicas of yourself.

Companies who want to be innovative need to promote a psychologically safe environment where creativity, exploring, trying *and sometimes making mistakes* are part of the culture.

Follow-up

Agree with the team member at the outset how you will hold them *accountable* and demand timely delivery in terms of milestones and target dates.

Ensure that you create a framework where the team member needs to come back to you as part of the follow-up so that you do not have to chase the deliverables.

Constructive feedback

Make sure your feedback is done in a timely manner and with the intention to develop your team member (not be hurtful). If the work delivered does not meet your expectations, strive to understand what the blocking factors are. Once you are both on the same page, let the team member correct the parts of the work that have not been satisfactory. (Do not take back the work and do it yourself!)

Praise good work

Remember to praise work that has been done well personally and in public when appropriate.

Please reflect and answer these questions in a separate note:
- **To be more effective in your delegation, which of the above points would you need to improve?**
- **What concrete actions do you plan to take as a result of your reflections?**
  (Identify actions for each of the delegation points you are seeking to improve)

About Tool 6.3 Effective Delegation

Effective delegation is an upfront investment that earns you time to work on priorities, while simultaneously developing competent teams who take ownership. By delegating you optimise your time and skills, enabling you to take yourself *and* your team to the next level. It is a win-win approach that ultimately benefits all parties involved.

Delegation may be simple in theory but few people are actually effective in practising it. This tool provides a useful checklist for effective delegation.

How to use the tool

The tool helps the coachee identify points they may have overlooked and highlights where they are struggling in their delegation. After briefly going through the points together, the coachee is asked to reflect by themselves as homework and bring their insights to the next coaching session to explore how they can optimise the way they delegate.

\>\>

To note:

Delegate to develop and empower team members. Extending trust is central to effective delegation. People develop, grow and thrive in environments where they are trusted and empowered to learn by doing. Lack of trust, however, is often an issue and when this is the case I challenge coachees to take a step back and ask themselves:

- Why don't I trust my team member(s)?
- Is it a question of their commitment or competence (see **Tool 1.10 Situational Leadership**) or is it about my own tendency to want to control everything?
- What do I need to be informed about and why?

Constructive feedback. If the coachee would benefit from support in this area I will refer to **Tool 1.17 Delivering Feedback**.

I also highlight the importance of not falling into the "It's quicker if I do it myself" trap. This links to the point about investing time in order to gain time. The consequence of the coachee being perceived as a 'safety net' for work that does not meet the expected outcome is that team members will not learn to do the work properly and the coachee will end up being burdened with tasks that should have been delegated.

"Focus on being productive instead of busy."

Tim Ferriss

6.4 Assess

Personal Efficiency and Effectiveness

It is a challenge to achieve satisfaction when we are constantly distracted from working on our priorities. The best way to find out how aligned (or misaligned) you are in relation to your priorities is to examine your calendar because it will help you to assess where you are placing your attention.

Refer to the Eisenhower Matrix as you go back over your calendar (last week(s), month).

Insert your answers directly under each question:

1. **How much of your time is spent on Important High tasks?** (top two quadrants)

---

2. **Of that time, how much is spent in the top left quadrant?** (yearly objectives, leadership, strategy, reflection, planning)

---

3. **If you have not spent sufficient time in the top left quadrant, what were the main obstacles for not achieving this?**

---

4. **What actions will you take to spend more time in the top left quadrant?**

About Tool 6.4 Assess

The coaching supports the coachee to put in place a structure that enables them to consistently operate in the top two quadrants of the Eisenhower Matrix, with a majority of time allocation in the upper left quadrant.

Nevertheless, even with the best structure it is easy to fall back into old habits from time to time. It is therefore useful to assess efficacy after a while and adjust if required.

How to use the tool

When it comes to how we spend our time, perception and reality are often misaligned. Scanning the calendar and answering the questions in the tool will give an accurate picture of what is going on and will help the coachee to assess what is working well and where adjustments need to be made.

"It's not always that we need to do more but rather that we need to focus on less."

Nathan W. Morris

— 6.5 Aide-Mémoire

Personal Efficiency and Effectiveness

Here are some practical reminders to help stay on track:

Priority Management
To keep your focus on priorities, refer regularly to the Eisenhower Matrix.

Weekly and Daily Planning
Block regular time in your calendar to plan the upcoming week(s).
Consider:
- ✓ *What commitments have been made?*
- ✓ *Is sufficient time blocked for the team?*
- ✓ *What work/meetings need preparation?*
- ✓ *What tasks need focused thinking time vs. focused work time?*
- ✓ *How much time will each task take? (time-realistic vs. time-optimistic)*
- ✓ *Is it important and/or urgent?*
- ✓ *When does it make most sense to do it?*
- ✓ *How much of my workload is unexpected (%) and do I take this into account in my planning?*
- ✓ *Should I be doing this task or can I delegate it?*
- ✓ *Have I blocked time for strategic thinking and to reflect on priorities?*

- Use your weekly plan as the reference and make a priority to-do list every day with maximum 10 points, starting with the highest priority task first.
- For work that requires concentration and focus, make sure to minimise interruptions and distractions.
- Before agreeing to take on additional work, assess it against your current plan and come back with a realistic timeframe - don't just say yes without considering the implications.
- Assess the alignment between what you are busy with against your planning on a regular basis. (perception vs. reality)

Procrastination
- Identify the tasks you are deliberately putting off and decide a time of the day when it makes most sense to get them done (most people prefer the start of the working day).
- Pick one or two of the most 'unpleasant' ones, tackle them and enjoy the difference that it makes to the rest of your day!!

Delegation
As you are picking up a new task, ask yourself:
- Should I be doing this?
- Could somebody else perform this task? Who?
- What would it entail if I were to delegate it?
- What would it give me in the longer term if I were to delegate this task?

Managing Emails

- Implement a 'cc folder' rule for incoming mails so that only the mails where you are a direct recipient are visible in your inbox.
- Schedule time slots each day to manage your emails to avoid looking at them constantly.
- To maximise efficiency, try to not open an email more than twice (the second time should be to action/delete/archive).

About Tool 6.5 Aide-Mémoire

Implementing new ways of working and making them a routine takes time and commitment. This tool serves as a *reminder* of central themes that have been worked on in the coaching sessions.

How to use the tool

This checklist tool is offered to the coaches in closing the coaching around personal efficiency and effectiveness.

Life Balance

"Don't confuse having a career
with having a life."

Hillary Clinton

About Life Balance

When I ask clients to describe what life balance is for them, many struggle to answer the question. Instead they proceed to tell me in fine detail what they *don't* want their life to be. Obviously, knowing what we don't want has a lot of value, but it is equally important to know what we *do* want - because to create a balanced life is to prioritise what is truly important to us. It means having the courage to make tough choices, set boundaries and take control, without apology or guilt.

When life is balanced we feel content with ourselves and the decisions we make. We are happier, healthier, better engaged and more resilient to stress. I prefer the term 'life balance' (as opposed to work/life balance) because I find it unnatural to separate work from life: work is an *integral part of life* and should feel purposeful and fulfilling as opposed to something that drains us.

Since life balance means living in alignment with our individual priorities, what we consider to be a 'balanced life' and how to create it can vary quite significantly from person to person. It is also worth noting that what we consider to be important at one point in time may change over the course of life's different phases. Life balance, as with most things, evolves and is therefore worth revisiting and re-evaluating on a regular basis.

The prevalent feeling among executives is that creating and maintaining a satisfactory life balance has become progressively challenging, and in my view there are three main reasons for this.

The first is not new: one of the main prerequisites for career advancement is a demonstration of commitment to work well beyond the standard 40-hour week. The second is that too many companies consistently expect employees to do the same - or more - work but with fewer resources. And the third is that technological progress has resulted in employees being in 'always on and reachable' mode, with the additional problems of widespread screen addiction and insufficient downtime for the brain. Unsurprisingly, these three reasons combined leave many people feeling overwhelmed and struggling to find mental and emotional equilibrium. This has serious health ramifications, something clearly evidenced by the alarming rate of burnout, as well as potentially fatal stress-related conditions such as early stroke and heart failure.

The system of more work with fewer resources was adopted during the global financial crisis of 2008/09. However, while cuts were absolutely necessary at the time, 'doing more with less' has somehow become today's *modus operandi*, despite profit levels back to normal (and sometimes even higher than before). It is thus not unusual to find senior executives being requested to take on several full-time roles with the expectation that they deliver outstanding results across all of them. But while it may be possible for one manager to work under unrealistic conditions and pressures in the short-term, it is not a sustainable 'business as usual' model.

In 2019 The World Health Organisation included burnout as an 'occupational phenomenon' in its *International Classification of Diseases,* and by doing so acknowledged it as being a global organisational problem. But until companies fully recognise this and create cultures where people are given the means to live balanced lives, employees are left with little choice but to take the matter into their own hands.

Working from home as a result of COVID-19 has brought a better life balance to many, but for others it has blurred the boundaries between private and work time as well as exacerbated pre-pandemic mental health issues and 'loneliness at work'. One positive outcome is that these topics are now part of the corporate conversation, and it is of the utmost importance that this continues and goes beyond just words to transform cultures that enable and support employees to live healthy and balanced lives.

"You can have it all.
You just can't have it all at once."

Oprah Winfrey

7.1 Current Situation

Life Balance

The first step in creating a balanced life is to understand where and how you are currently spending your time. Once you have this clarity, you can decide if the current situation is satisfactory or if you wish to re-distribute the time you have at your disposal.

When you become more aware about potential areas of neglect, you can take concrete steps to integrate those areas and bring about a better life balance.

Question:
Does the distribution of time illustrated below reflect my current life situation?

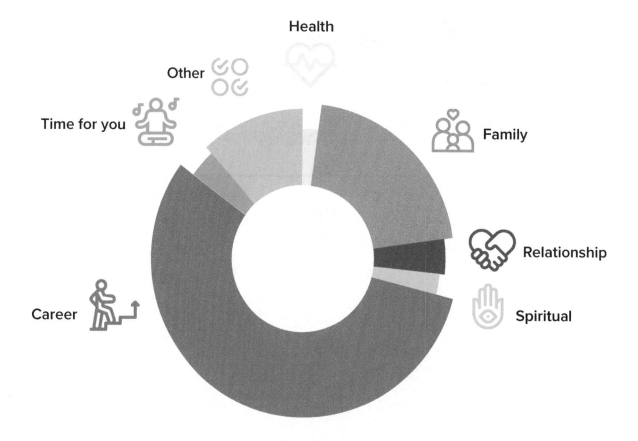

About Tool 7.1 Current Situation

For many of us time is an elusive concept, and this helps to explain why the *perception* and *reality* of how we spend our time often differ; and when we reflect about life as a whole with its many different aspects, it can also feel difficult to grasp. This is why we must first understand our current life balance situation before taking actions to improve it.

To achieve life balance, we need to harmonise all the aspects we consider important in such a way that life feels meaningful and complete - because when we live more holistically we also feel more whole ourselves. To facilitate clearer thinking it is therefore helpful to separate the different aspects, examine each of them and then consolidate them to assess our life in its entirety.

In this tool, the different life aspects are *Career*, *Health* (e.g. fitness, diet), *Family*, *Relationships* (e.g. friends, social networks), *Spiritual* (e.g. meditation, religion), *Time for You* (e.g. recover, fun, hobbies) and *Other* (e.g. household, personal administration). Certain aspects may overlap or mean different things to different people, for instance some may consider *Family* and *Time for You* to be the same.

How to use the tool

To uncover their current situation, the coachee is requested to analyse a typical week in their life. The analysis consists of distributing their time across a 105-hour week (7 x 15-hour days) as things currently stand, using the prescribed seven life aspects.

Once they have completed their analysis I will create a pie chart for the upcoming coaching session. Pie charts are very useful in this context to help the coachee relate more easily to the different aspects and connect to reality. I will ask if the pie chart accurately reflects the coachee's current situation, which serves as a good starting point to explore what is going on.

The pie chart illustration above shows what a 60-hour working week can look like in relation to the other aspects of life. However, life balance is not just about time distribution: it is also about what is going on inside each pie slice. It is often assumed that putting in too many hours at the office is the sole cause of work-related burnout; however, while it is proven that the risk of burnout increases significantly when the working week starts to exceed fifty hours, what actually causes it is more complex. Burnout actually has more to do with *how* people experience their time at work, and some of the main psychological stressors are:

- Unmanageable workload
- Unrealistic time pressures
- Uncertainty
- Perceived lack of control
- Isolation

Similarly, from a private life perspective the hours in the *Family* slice may seem satisfactory to the coachee, but if those hours are spent exhausted on the sofa instead of being present with loved ones, this is something they will probably want to change.

It is important to be mindful about all aspects of the current situation in order to fully understand what is going on for the coachee, both professionally and privately.

If the coachee wants to create a better balance by reducing the hours in the *Career* slice, I may refer to **Tool 6.1 Eisenhower Matrix** as well as other tools in the Toolkit that may be relevant once a proper diagnosis of the issue has been made. These could include **Tools 6.2 Checkpoint, 6.3 Effective Delegation, 1.6 Role Clarification, 2.8 and 2.9 Assertiveness** (to push back or say no) in order to help the coachee devise an appropriate strategy.

"When you say yes to others, make sure you are not saying no to yourself."

Paolo Coelho

"Self-care is giving the world the best of you, instead of what's left of you."

Katie Reed

7.2 What is Important to You?

Life Balance

Reflect on the current Life Balance pie chart you have received from your coach and answer the following questions:

1. **What does life balance mean for me?**

2. **Am I living a balanced life?**

3. **Which parts of my life are important to preserve?**

4. **What brings me joy?**

5. **Am I prioritising what is truly important for me in my private life?**
   (If not, then what is holding me back?)

6. **Am I involved in too many things?** (work and private)

7. **How do I manage the stress in my life?**

8. **What do I do to take care of myself?** (recover, restore and recharge)

9. **What are the things I am grateful for in my life?**

10. **What do I want to start doing?**

11. **What do I want to stop doing?**

About Tool 7.2 What is Important to You?

While a balanced life means prioritising what is important, it is also essential to understand the critical part that self-care plays in creating that balance. Self-care is the intentional act of looking after oneself and nurturing one's wellbeing in order to have a content mind and a healthy body.

The questions in this tool encourage profound holistic thinking to help devise life balance strategies that are relevant and lasting.

How to use the tool

Building on the previous **Tool 7.1 Current Situation**, the coachee is asked to reflect and complete the questions in this tool prior to the coaching session. For many this is a useful but difficult exercise because it often brings forth insights that can be hard to face - particularly if there has been neglect in certain cherished aspects. The coach needs to apply the right mix of sensitivity, empathy and assertiveness to support the coachee in their exploration.

To note:

Question 5. We sometimes need reminding that we have *choice*. To create life balance, certain choices may not be easy but may nevertheless be necessary, and to delve deeper I often ask the coachee: *Does where you are choosing to place your attention match your intention?* The deliberate use of the word *choosing* fosters a sense of self-empowerment within the coachee and helps motivate them to take charge of their situation.

Question 6. When we are involved in too many things it is easy to lose sight of what really matters. There is great value in considering what can be simplified and/or eliminated to gain more time, space and peace for those aspects we value most.

Question 8. Far too many executives score poorly on self-care: they simply do not prioritise their wellbeing. There is a false notion among some that prioritising wellbeing is somehow selfish considering all the demands on their time; however, the truth is that prioritising one's wellbeing is the *opposite* of selfishness. If this is this case I ask them: *How can you be the best version of yourself - an authentic, resourceful and engaged leader and colleague (not to mention parent, partner and friend) - if you don't take time to recover, restore and recharge?*

An outstanding metaphor for this is the oxygen mask drill on an aeroplane. I remember how astonished I was as a young girl the first time I heard the adult instructed to put on their mask *before* tending to the child. Indeed, it came across as totally selfish! But when I understood that the adult would be of little or no help to the child without sufficient oxygen himself, it made perfect sense. Putting on our own unique 'oxygen mask', whatever that may be, is necessary to build the mental strength and wellbeing required to be the best versions of ourselves in a time where the requirement to adapt is unremitting.

Question 9. Practising gratitude on a regular basis is proven to have a positive impact on mental and physical health: it helps both to reduce stress and increase happiness. When we feel gratitude, natural endorphins (the 'feel good' chemicals) are released into the blood stream which then strengthens our immune system. These endorphins are highly effective in helping us cope with stress and counter negative emotions such as anxiety and depression. Psychological stressors (see examples in the text box in **Tool 7.1 Current Situation**) produce cortisol in our bodies, which is harmful over time and if unmanaged can cause persistent symptoms such as mental and physical exhaustion, insomnia, short-term memory loss and a reduced capacity to think clearly.

>>

When we start to pay attention we realise that there is much to be grateful for. By deliberately tapping into feelings of genuine gratitude, we can use our own natural endorphins as energy boosters to proactively and better manage our internal state. This is such a powerful means of self-care that if it resonates with coachees I encourage them to include a daily gratitude practice into their life balance action plan.

Questions 10 and 11. Once the coachee has identified what they want to start and stop doing, it is important that these steps are specific and actionable, preferably with target dates for each to ensure accountability. Identified start and stop points are largely about changing habits but those changes are seldom major. Small tweaks and adjustments should not be underestimated as they can be considerable game-changers.

"Better learn balance. Balance is key."

Mr. Miyagi

7.3 Desired Life Balance

Life Balance

As you review your desired hourly distribution in the pie chart below, consider this question:

Is it in line with your expectations?

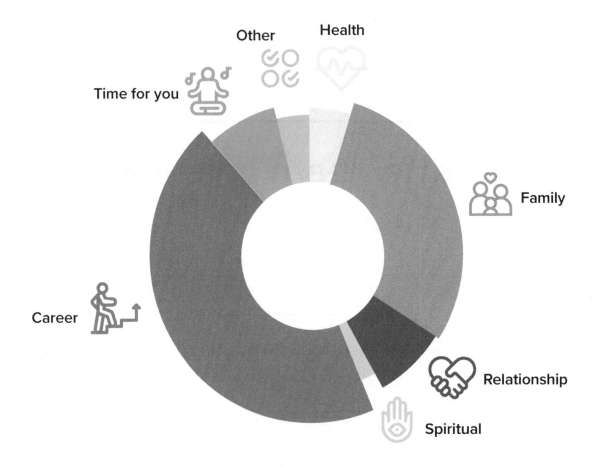

Go back over your answers in the document *What is Important to You*?

Reflect on the following questions and answer in a separate note:

1. **In addition to those actions identified in questions 10 and 11, are any others required for you to move from your Current Situation to your Desired Situation?**
If yes, what are they?

2. **How will you ensure that you to stick to your plan?**

About Tool 7.3 Desired Life Balance

Most of us want to be more present, calm and connected in the moment. This happens when our *attention* (where we place our focus) is aligned with our *intention* (our priorities), be it with our partner, children, friends, colleagues or clients. It happens when we are in equilibrium with our principles and those aspects we value the most.

How to use the tool

Once the coachee has completed **Tool 7.2 What is Important to You?** I ask them to revisit their current hourly distribution (**Tool 7.1 Current Situation**) and make any adjustments they deem necessary to achieve their desired life balance. Based on their update, I produce a new 'desired' pie chart for the upcoming coaching session. Together we contrast the new pie chart with the original and revisit the coachee's identified stop and start actions. The pie chart in this tool shows what an adjusted distribution of a 45-hour working week can look like.

I have seen a large variety of pie chart constellations and would like to emphasise that there is no ideal distribution that suits everyone: one person's life balance is not another's and individuals handle stress to differing degrees. It is therefore vital that the coach is sensitive to the needs and wants of the coachee, in particular when they do not resonate with those of the coach.

Balancing the jigsaw puzzle of life requires careful deliberation. Priorities, preferences and choices will depend on people's personality types as well as where they are in their career cycle, what is expected of their role/position, the organisation's corporate culture and the demands of their own family or personal circle.

In this fast-paced and productivity-focused world, taking time to revitalise and recharge one's batteries is more important than ever: taking care of oneself is not a *luxury* but a *necessity*. Because self-care is such a critical piece in the life balance equation, I make absolutely sure that it is part of the coaching conversation; and since self-care means different things to different people, coachees might allocate it in *Time for You, Health, Family* and/or *Spiritual*. If coachees feel challenged by this concept, I encourage suggesting simple things that resonate with them and that are easy to incorporate: listening to relaxing music, walking in nature, getting sufficient sleep, detoxing from social media, meditating, practising gratitude, connecting with loved ones and friends, or even taking time out to do nothing.

When we know what we are aiming to achieve, it is imperative to incorporate identified activities (exercise, date nights, quality family time, meditation) into the calendar and *commit to the plan* - because it is too easy to get side-tracked. The commitment helps to ensure that work does not come *before* self-care.

We do well to remember that creating a balanced life is not something we do once and then sit back expecting it to maintain itself: it is something we need to continuously monitor and keep adjusting as circumstances change and life evolves.

Appendix

Coaching Questions

Intention questions:

- What specifically do you want to achieve?
- What would the ideal outcome be?
- What do you really want?
- How will you know when you have succeeded?

Clarifying questions:

- What is currently happening?
- Say more... *
- How was your experience?
- What is the hardest/most challenging part of this for you?
- Where did it go wrong?
- How would you like it to be?
- What do you know now that you did not know before?
- What did that mean to you?
- How would you have liked to behave?
- What might you do differently next time?
- Where will that get you?
- What was important about that?
- What did you learn from that?
- What made you choose that?
- How have you coped in the past?
- What does X mean to you?
- When did it start?
- When did you realise.....?
- When did you decide.....?
- When you say .... what do you mean?
- What does .... mean to you?
- And...? *
- So...? *
- Because... *
- Is that paraphrased correctly?
- What specifically?
- How would you summarise what you have just said in one sentence?
- From your boss's/team's perspective, what might they be experiencing here?

* use the tone of your voice to encourage the coachee to explore further

Challenging questions:

- What is *really* going on?
- What does that tell you about yourself?
- What prevents you from achieving X?
- What would you do if there were no barriers?

- What is the evidence for this? Is it an interpretation or a fact?
- Can you be certain that this will happen?
- What other choices do you have?
- What's another way/perspective to explore your situation?
- What is the bigger picture here?
- What would the ideal situation or working relationship be like?
- What would you gain/lose by doing/saying that?
- Describe your experience if someone said/did that to you.
- What are the potential consequences for you and/or others?
- What advice would you give to a friend in a similar situation?
- Everyone?
- Always? Can you think of an exception?
- Never?
- Nobody?
- What is so terrible about:
    - being wrong sometimes?
    - not having all the answers?
    - not knowing something?
- How might this be an opportunity for learning about yourself and/or others?

Reframe to possibilities:

- Describe a time when this wasn't an issue for you.
- Have you overcome similar issues in the past?
- How did you feel then?
- What was your life like then?
- What strengths helped you to get through that time?
- What strategies did you use to deal with the situation?
- What resources did you rely on?
- What strengths do you have that you're not using now?
- Where can you start to make a change?

Identifying options:

- What have you tried so far?
- What has worked and what has not?
- How is this similar to or different from the way you have approached this in the past?
- What are some options to consider?
- Who can you ask for help/support?
- What other resources do you need moving forward?
- And what else could you do?

Action questions:

- What action would you like to take around that?
- How will you do that in order to achieve the best possible results?
- How many?
- How much?
- How often?
- Is there anything else you need to do before that?
- What else do you need to ensure you move forward?

- What will your next step be?
- When will you do that?

Commitment questions:

- How committed are you to taking that action? (scale of 1-10 or %)
- How important is this to you?
- How do you feel about doing that?
- What would need to happen in order to raise your commitment?

Permission questions:

- Can I share with you what's coming to my mind?
- May I add to what you have just said?
- Would it be useful to brainstorm this point?

Resources

If you are interested in downloading the tools in this book, I invite you to visit **www.coachdynamix.com**.

If you want to follow me, I would love to connect with you on LinkedIn.

About the Author

Monica Jonsson pioneered the corporate coaching sector in Luxembourg and is founder of the country's first and leading coaching practice, CoachDynamix (2003).

Based in Luxembourg, she delivers one-to-one, team and group corporate coaching services to senior executives and entrepreneurs in the global business community. With more than 80 client companies spanning across a diversity of industries, she has a profound insight into the comprehensive range of issues companies face in an ever-changing business landscape.

Monica is an accredited Master Coach by the International Authority for Professional Coaching & Mentoring (IAPC&M). She has a master's in Neuro-Linguistic Programming (NLP) and has trained in systemic coaching and constellations, neuroscience, emotional intelligence, group mastery, clean language and transpersonal coaching. She also holds a degree in economics from the University of Stockholm.

She has worked in predominantly international environments in Sweden, Hong Kong and Luxembourg. Prior to becoming a coach she worked in the telecommunications sector for Telia (Sweden), Hongkong Telecom, MACH and IBM. Her experience covers a variety of areas including strategic consulting, marketing, sales, service development and supplier management.

In addition to her work as a coach, Monica moderates and participates in panel discussions with senior corporate executives to raise awareness around the importance of leadership and gender balance.

For more information about CoachDynamix and the coaching services offered, please visit www.coachdynamix.com.

Made in the USA
Coppell, TX
09 September 2023

21417352R00155